Getting Even

Getting Even

The Complete Book of Dirty Tricks

GEORGE HAYDUKE

LYLE STUART INC.   SECAUCUS, N.J.

This book is dedicated to three people who have had a profound influence on my activism.

First, Edward Abbey, who gave me my literary life in his classic The Monkey Wrench Gang, *probably knew it would come to this. This book is also dedicated to the spirit of Howard Beal, a brilliant characterization by Paddy Chayefsky in his screenplay for* Network. *And I owe a lot to Peder Lund. He's my friend.*

Queries regarding rights and permissions
should be addressed to Lyle Stuart Inc.,
120 Enterprise Ave., Secaucus, N.J. 07094.

Published by Lyle Stuart Inc. Published
simultaneously in Canada by Musson Book Co.,
a division of General Publishing Co. Limited,
Don Mills, Ontario.

Manufactured in the United States of America

ISBN 0-8184-0314-4

Contents

Preface

Jimmy Carter, a president, invited Leonid Brezhnev to the White House for an evening of the usual state activities. As part of the entertainment, Carter invited Brezhnev to sit down at the official White House piano and play a dirge of the Volga or the Fall of Leningrad.

As Brezhnev sat down to play, he could not help but notice a red button at the end of the keyboard. Unable to restrain his curiosity, he pushed the button. Immediately, from the ceiling directly above, a large sliding door opened and a huge cascade of water was dumped on the Soviet leader's head.

The White House occupants and their staff laughed and laughed.

The months passed, and Leonid Brezhnev dried off and licked the SALT in his wounds. It came to pass then that he had occasion to invite Jimmy Carter to the official Red Residence in the Kremlin. After a fine repast, the official Red Square piano rolled in on its halftracks.

"Sit down and play a born-again-Baptist hymn for us," Brezhnev asked gently. As he poised to play, Mr. Carter noticed a small red button at the end of the keyboard. Curiosity was too much for the old Georgia boy, and he pushed the button.

Nothing happened.

The Kremlin crew guffawed, roared, snorted, and

playfully punched one another's shoulders in obvious glee.

Carter was puzzled. He appealed to Brezhnev, "Tell me, please—what amuses you and your staff so much? I mean, there was no water or anything. What is so amusing? Please tell me, so I can share your unique Soviet humor with my fellow-Americans back in the United States."

Leonid Brezhnev smiled. "What United States?"

> Thanx and a tip of the
> trickster's hat to
> world traveler Rog Axford

Without Whom...

There would be no book like this if there were not a lot of really frustrated and angry people, many of whom have contributed to this effort. As you might suspect, most of these people did not want to be mentioned by name or even hinted at in the book for fear of retribution, legal or otherwise. I have already thanked each of these honest people individually. Therefore, when names are mentioned in this book, they are probably not the real names of the people involved—with the exception of public figures, of course.

I owe a lot to the following: former employees of and independent contractors to the CIA, DEA, FBI, MI6, and NSA; Nellie Gaydosh; Andrew Grezniak; Peder Lund; Neil Price; Donald Segretti; Dana Spiardi; Dick Tuck; and the Yippie defense minister.

We all owe a lot to these pioneers: Lenny Bruce; Dick Gregory; Abbie Hoffman; Julius Hoffman; Jerry Rubin; Mort Sahl.

Perhaps when you finish this book you would wish to join the fine people whose names and references appear on this gratitude page. If you have some dirty tricks to share with me for volume 2, please jot them down and send them along to me, care of Lyle Stuart Inc., 120 Enterprise Avenue, Secaucus, N.J. 07094.

Introduction

The revolutionary Carlos Hassler shouted his rallying war cry, "Break General Motors down to private!" However, you can be sure as inflation that the power establishment, including the courts and regulatory agencies, aren't at all interested in breaking up or down their buddies. As Rudy Molnar, president of the independent Pennsylvania/Delaware Service Station Dealers Association, said, "All we get from the government is lies and bullshit. They're working for the major oil companies."

Molnar, one of the most honest-spoken and ethical men I've ever seen in action, is a dedicated small-business man. He is the real-life model for the American ethic and dream. As you know, the oil-company cartel and its governmental lover have turned Molnar's dream and our lives into a living nightmare.

Small America—the powerless middle class—is being screwed all over. They have no representation, no champion, and no protection from this plundering. The law? According to the criminologist Doctor Joseph Bogan, a former beat cop and officer, "There is no real justice in America for the little guy. He goes to court knowing he's right. Yet, *boom!* . . . the bad guy wins. The deck is stacked against the little guy. He's a loser."

One hero, Howard Beal of *Network,* says it all: "I'm

mad as hell, and I'm not going to take this any more!" By inference, the only option left for the little guy is to use dirty tricks.

Dirty tricks have become an operational alternative because Middle America's other options have been shut down. Who does governmental regulation and bureaucracy hurt? Where is competition? After we get off Main Street and leave the independent small-business man, the mom 'n' pop businesses, and the folks trying to make it on less than ten thousand dollars a year, we've lost touch with capitalism.

Where do we find free competition?

Not in aerospace, airlines, the auto industry, banking, or agribusiness. There's no competition in chemicals, medical drugs, lumber, or lightbulbs. There is no real competition in steel, energy, utilities, or armament. The idea of America as a free-enterprise, free-market system is a myth, clouded by large government and international cartels.

William Winpisinger, president of the Machinists Union, says, "One more turn of the screw by either the corporate establishment or the bureaucratic government, and the working people, poor people, and retired people of this country are going to rebel."

The first wave of this rebellion lies in striking back at these forces which dictate our lives—getting even for the frustrations, fears, and discomfort they cause us.

This is a book about dirty tricks. They go beyond the realm of even the most hardcore practical jokes. But they are not to be taken seriously or pursued actively. People who ignore this directive could spend time in jail—or worse.

In other words, this book is for your amusement, nothing else. Fantasize to your heart's content—but if you put these ideas into practice, you do so at your own risk and against the warnings of the publisher and the author.

There must be an acceptable motive for such operational vengeance. Minor annoyances build up. For example, we all have been kept waiting at the other end of a silent telephone line for many long minutes, only to be told by a care-less clerk that the person to whom we wish to speak is not available. Try that on long distance. Almost all of us have been swindled to some degree by a mail-order firm that refuses to answer complaint letters, despite federal laws that say they must. What do you do when a computer keeps adding interest to your bill each month when you paid the entire amount ninety days earlier? How do you rid yourself of the feeling caused by these escalating annoyances?

Maybe you've been the victim of false or careless reporting or misinformation on an insurance or credit investigation. The federal laws allow you to check your files at local credit bureaus and certain insurance- and medical-record facilities. Doing so, people are shocked to find slanderously false information about themselves in these files. In many cases, this false information has been used to deny people loans, insurance, jobs, and promotions. What can you do beyond helplessly rely on more bureaucracy, inane and often contradictory regulations, and the further frustration of "going through channels"?

Gail Penga spent thousands of dollars to go through four years of college, compiling a 3.6 average and hopes for a bright career and future. Two weeks from graduation she was told by the college's registrar that she would not receive her diploma because she had inadvertently taken an incorrect course. She said that her academic advisor, a Professor Savant, had given her a verbal order to take the course.

The system closed ranks to protect itself from the complaint of an ordinary mortal like a student. The advisor and the registrar held a meeting with an assistant dean and decreed that the student was disbelieved. Period. The registrar, a surly sort, even gave her hell for being so stupid as to take the course in the first place, then to question the wisdom of the system after the fact.

"If you want to graduate, you come back here in the fall and take that proper course—and pay for it, too," the registrar told her.

Forget job hunting and that career for a while, Gail. You've just been had, and all the avenues of appeal have been shut down by administrative fiat.

By now, the gentle reader is thinking, There has to be a law. Perhaps there is, but that calls for a lawyer. Lawyers cost money. If you're screaming for *justice* for Gail, remember that justice is slow, costly, and often unfair to little people.

Gail had a better idea. She got one of her sexier female friends to visit Professor Savant, her old academic advisor, in his office and at the union coffee shop, and to walk around campus with him. High visibility of the couple was the idea. Several of Gail's other friends started a rumor about this co-ed–professor affair, and the rumor spread very quickly and credibly on the small campus.

Posing enthusiastically as the advisor's lover, Gail's friend was blushingly coy about the "affair." The man was unaware of the romantic angle and ignorant of the rumors, simply pleased that such a charming, lovely young woman would show personal interest in his boring life.

When another of Gail's friends telephoned Professor Savant's wife to do her duty and tell the "wronged" woman about the "other" woman, the ersatz lover suddenly dropped all contact with the bewildered academic. Within two days, another of Gail's friends called the man's wife and, using the name of a well-known co-ed callus-back, pleaded with the woman to stop her husband from making sexual advances to her and her co-ed friends.

Gail explained her thinking: "That advisor screwed up my life with his bad counseling; then he lied about it. I just returned the favor with a little tighter twist of the screw, if you'll excuse the imagery."

A good point may be taken from Gail's program, and that is, the best plans for getting even involve irony—the vengeance should fit the original act. For instance, an old country fellow we'll call Leatherstocking used to poach a deer or five strictly for food. Trying to live on his meager Social Security check, the old man had little spare change for high-priced supermarket meat. His nosy neighbor, a wealthy antihunter, reported Leatherstocking's poaching to the district game protector. Now, this young game protector knew Leatherstocking's plight and needs, so he had always turned his head when the old-timer shot an extra deer on his own property. But because of the nosy neighbor's complaint, the official had to talk to the old man, an embarrassment for both of them.

His duty done, the game protector put the issue from his mind. Leatherstocking did not. Using an illegal homemade silencer on his rifle, Leatherstocking went out the following week and quietly and carefully took four deer. He dressed and skinned them, hiding the meat safely away for his future use. That night, he took the fresh deer hides to the nosy neighbor's home. All was quiet as the old man carefully unsnapped the tarp covering the bed of the nosy neighbor's truck, placed the hides in the truck bed, and covered them with newspapers. He replaced the tarp, and within ten minutes he was at home on the telephone with a trusted friend, also an old-timer.

A few moments later, the telephone rang at the game protector's place. It was the other old-timer calling.

"I'm going to have to do my civic duty about this hypocritical antihunter and report Mr. Nosy Neighbor for poaching. He has this pickup truck, and . . ."

I'll let your imagination and sense of justice supply the rest.

Dirty tricks are probably older than people. But one favorite involved a very minor royal figure from tenth- or eleventh-century England. He was King Ironside, and that really was his name. One of his obviously mortal enemies, a chap named Edrick, mounted a crossbow underneath the seat of the royal privy. The bow was fired by a very elementary pressure trigger activated by weight pushing down on the seat. A historian of that period titled the story

"The Arrow That Does Not Miss." It's a very fundamental and true story of just how far the oppressed will go to deal with their oppressors.

Kwame Nkrumah, a national hero to many people in his native Ghana, was educated in the United States. But he learned most of his political science the hard way, as a pawn of the superpowers playing games with his nonaligned nation. He wrote an excellent manual called *Handbook of Revolutionary Warfare*, a portion of which is devoted to propaganda. He writes:

"An indispensable preliminary to battle is to attack the mind of the enemy, to undermine the will to fight so that the result of the battle is decided before the fighting begins. The revolutionary army attacks an irresolute and demoralized army."

He wrote those words even before the United States got kicked out of Vietnam. You can use his philosophy in your dirty-tricks war against those big bullies of our own nation. Our own recent history gives us adequate documentation of how it works.

In the sixties, protestors were told to work for change within the system. This is farcical, because our system is a bureaucracy, and there is never a significant change within a bureaucracy. As William Powell points out in *The Anarchist Cookbook*, "There is no justice in bureaucracy for the individual, for bureaucracy caters only to itself." Further, he wrote, "One cannot practice the same bureaucracy one is fighting against."

Every time the establishment puts its heavy foot down on some suffering Middle American, another potential rebel is recruited. For example, Peter Brownstein, a New Jersey man, happened to be peacefully installing a burglar alarm that would ring directly in township-police headquarters if anyone tried to break into the legal gun collection held in his home. At that very moment township police, who admitted later that they acted on a bad tip, raided Brownstein's apartment.

They seized his entire collection without allowing a

word of civil protest. Brownstein, who must be a fairly cool man, allowed the farce to go to the Middlesex County grand jury, which failed to indict the legal collector. The county prosecutor even pointed out that everything Brownstein owned was legal.

Why in hell did the police make that raid? What if Brownstein had lost in court? Would you trust a jury of your peers to make an important decision on your future, such as whether that future would be free? There has to be a better way.

Robert Townsend, a truly enlightened man of many corporate talents, presents an excellent rationale for the motives behind the methods presented in this book. He notes, "The one thing the Establishment is prepared for is violent frontal attack. They may have pure lard inside, but they've got twenty-four inches of armor plate in front." Avoid frontal attack.

Some readers may wish this book had more compromise and a stronger lean toward concilation. Those inclined toward mediation will suggest that this book moves directly to the kick in the crotch or the kidney thrust. That's very observant of them. The bibliography of this volume documents a variety of very worthy books that cover the more gentle methods of getting your own way. Some of these fine books outline dirty tricks, harassment techniques, and practical jokes. The book you are reading now starts off with the premise that the situation is beyond these more gentle methods of resolve.

As that genteel statesman and land speculator Barry Goldwater once noted, "Extremism in the defense of liberty is no vice." That's cogent advice as you read these pages. The stories on these pages are meant for the reader who has had it up to his or her craw with mediation, compromise, and turning the other cheek.

A trickster would tell an ageless senior citizen to put a big staple in the middle of his IRS 1040 short-form IBM card, spray paint some bureaucrat's limousine windshield, know that a gallon of Karo in the fuel tank of a D9 will slow down the land rape of a coal stripper or natural-gas company.

To call upon Yippie Jerry Rubin, "A society which suppresses adventure makes the only adventure the suppression of that society."

That reminds me of Richard Nixon and his band of merry tricksters. Bob Haldeman looked hard at political practical joker Dick Tuck. It was May 5, 1973, during the National Watergate Extravaganza. In his best prescandal snarl, old crewcut Bob barked, "You son of a bitch, you started all this."

Smiling harmlessly, the calm Tuck replied, "Yeah, Bob, but you guys ran it into the ground."

General Advice

Throughout this book, I make many references to the mark, which is a street label hung on the victim of a scam or con. In our case, the mark is a bureaucrat, civil servant, lawyer, cop, businessperson, military officer, government official, teacher, merchant, manager, employer, employee, or other person who has done something unpleasant to you, your family, your property, or your friends. Never think of a mark as the victim of dirty tricks. Think of the mark as a very deserving target.

Before you read any of the specific areas of this book, please read these next few vital paragraphs. They tell how a trickster prepares before going into action.

1. PREPARE A PLAN.

Plan all details before you take any action at all. Don't even ad-lib something from this book without a plan of exactly what you're going to do and how. If your campaign involves a series of actions, make a chronological chart, then coordinate your efforts. Make a list of possible problems. Plan what you'll do if you get caught—depending upon who catches you. You must have every option, contingency, action, reaction, and evaluation planned in advance.

2. GATHER INTELLIGENCE.

Play like a real intelligence operative and compile a file on your mark. How detailed and thorough you are depends upon your plans for the mark. For a simple get-even number, you obviously need less intelligence than if you're planning an involved, time-release campaign. Before you start spying, make a written list of all the important things you need to know about the target—be it a person, a company, or an institution.

3. BUY AWAY FROM HOME.

Any supplies, materials, or services you need must be purchased away from where you live. Buy way in advance and pay in cash. Try to be as inconspicuous and colorless as possible. Don't talk unnecessarily with people. The best rule here is a spook's favorite—a good agent will get lost in a crowd of one. The idea is for people not to remember you.

4. NEVER TIP YOUR HAND.

Don't get cocky, cute, 'n' clever and start dropping hints about who's doing what to whom. I know that sounds stupid, but some would-be tricksters are gabby. Of course, in some of the cases this will not apply, for example, unselling car customers at the dealership or other tricks in which the scenario demands your personal involvement.

5. NEVER ADMIT ANYTHING.

If accused, act shocked, hurt, outraged, or amused, whichever seems most appropriate. Deny everything, unless, again, your plan involves overt personal involvement. If you're working covert, stay that way. The only cool badass out of Watergate was Gordon Liddy, and he kept his mouth shut.

6. NEVER APOLOGIZE; IT'S A SIGN OF WEAKNESS.

Normally, harassment of a citizen is a low-priority case with the police. The person's priority increases along with his socio-financial position in the community and with his political connections. If you are at war with a corporation, utility, or institution, that's a different ball game. They often have private security people, sometimes retired federal or state investigators. So by habit, these people may not play according to the law either. If you play dirty tricks upon a governmental body, be prepared to have a case opened. But how hard it is followed depends upon a lot of factors. Understanding all this ahead of time is part of your intelligence planning before you get started in action. The best advice I can offer is to know the law, know your rights, know the risks, weigh the risks, plan everything ahead of time in detail, be careful, and don't get caught. If you do get caught, don't admit anything to anyone . . . maybe not even to your lawyer. He may not want to know anyway.

As a cautionary note, I should tell you that in the summer of 1979, federal authorities in Pennsylvania opened an investigation into a series of harassing actions against a Pittsburgh attorney. The attorney's friends and colleagues received a letter suggesting that the mark was a homosexual and a pornographer. The evidence indicates that the attorney is innocent of the slanderous charges. He blamed the bogus letter on a disgruntled former client.

This book has been simply organized by topical heading, which is by no means inclusive or even logical. You can use the table of contents as an index if you wish. Because the topical areas are often cross-indexed in content if not in tactic, materials, or form, it may be helpful to check headings related to your special interest. In a few cases I have done some in-text cross-indexing for you. But before you go to the topical areas, please read these next few pages of rambling explanation, too. It is vital to know all the ground rules.

Caution

Caution

Caution

The schemes presented in this book have been suggested by people who have actually used them. Many of these people have asked to have their names changed or altered. Some sources have asked that I use totally fictional names. I did so to protect good people, maybe at the expense of bad people. However, the tricks, scams, stunts, cons, and scenarios presented here are given for *informational and amusement purposes only.* It is not my intent that you use this book as a manual or as a trickster's cookbook. I certainly don't expect that anyone who reads this book would actually ever *do* any of the things described here . . . .

This book is written to entertain and inform readers, not to persuade them to commit an illegal act. I am personally a very pacifistic person, so I could hardly advocate something I did not personally believe in. From my own mild disposition, I could hardly tell someone else to make any of these tactics operational. To do that would be hypocritical, and I am no hypocrite. Actually, I am a registered Republican, and I play on a church-league softball team.

Please read this book with that proper reference in mind. I do not want to be responsible for the personal or corporate suffering of anyone, regardless of how deserved that suffering would be. There is a cynic's version of the

Golden Rule that goes, "Do unto others as they have done unto you." Nastier cynics modify that to read, "Do unto others before they do unto you." Not being a cynic, I try to live by the real Golden Rule.

Happy reading, and remember, please, *all this is just in good, clean fun!*

Additives

Harmful additives are a formidable weapon against machinery, people, and processes. Additives perform one or more of the following:

1. Corrosion . . . sulfuric acid, for example, will corrode the gutter, eaves, and downspout of a home; dumped salt will mar a building surface or floor and kill a lawn.

2. Contamination . . . copper salts will rot rubber products; soap in a public or corporate fountain will create giant foam. Or put it in a steam boiler if you're more serious about the matter.

3. Abrasion . . . introduction of light, coarse materials, such as resins, to automotive fuel, or metal filings placed in the gears of industrial machinery, will create frictional havoc.

4. Impurities . . . adding sugar to gasoline creates harmful carbon from the burning sugar, stopping the engine.

Soaps and detergents make wonderful additions to food and could even be beneficial if the target happens to be constipated. If not, then soap-laden munchies or drinks will really keep him moving.

During my stay as an invited guest of Uncle Sam I recall some dirty tricksters' making an action statement against being on KP. They liberally coated various pans and cooking vessels with GI soap. They washed mugs with a lot of soap, then neglected to rinse them before letting the utensils dry. Later, when some drinkable potion like milk or coffee was poured into the mug by some unsuspecting mark, the soap was activated. *Woosh!*

Soap is also a very effective additive to containers in which food is prepared. The secret is to disguise the taste. Various other additives will do that and other tricks.

A horny old pharmacist, Doctor Frank Pittlover, claims there really is a working aphrodisiac. His is almost as esoteric as the fake stuff you read about in men's magazines. Here's what Doctor Pittlover says: "It's known as yohimbine hydrochloride (C_{21}, H_{26}, O_3N_2), an obscure sex stimulant that operates on the central nervous system. It was the aphrodisiac used by the CIA in their MK/ULTRA scam." It is not on the Controlled Substances Act list—yet—and it is classed as a "veterinary aphrodisiac." That means you can get it openly from a pharmaceutical-supply source. What you do with it after you get it is probably your own business.

There are other references to and uses of additives in many other topical areas of this book . . . many more than could be indexed here.

"Take tea and see" is a good advertising slogan that should also alert the dirty trickster to some additives brought to our attention by herbal-tea producers. Two common products of many herbal teas have side effects that the true trickster could define only as delightful. First, some teas contain the leaves, flowers, and bark of the senna plant, a tropical shrub related to our bean plant. The dried leaves, bark, and flowers of this plant are a mighty powerful laxative. Chamomile flowers are also popular in herbal teas. Related to ragweed and goldenrod, chamomile can produce severe reactions in people sensitive to plants of that family.

The trick in both cases is to obtain extracts of both products and use them in concentrated enough additive form to create the desired effect.

Meanwhile, from the other end, Doctor Christopher Garwood Doyle has a prescription that could really get a mark moving. Syrup of ipecac is a common purgative, easily available. Here's how Doctor Doyle uses it.

"Your mark is with you or your agent somewhere having a few drinks," the doctor outlines. "Presumably, the mark is drinking something sweet and heavy, like rum and Coke. When the mark goes to the bathroom or is otherwise out of the area, mix one tablespoon of syrup of ipecac in with the drink.

"You now have a fifteen-minute waiting—or escaping, if you prefer—period for the mixture to get active. After that, bombs away! The mark will begin violent projectile vomiting, which really messes up the nearby environment and anyone else who happens to be in the way.

"We first did this in medical school, using it to get back at a classmate who'd turned us in to officials for having an after-hours party in our dorm with women and booze. They threw the book at us because we were supposed to be mature medical students.

"The kid who did this fancied himself a real boozer," Doctor Doyle explained, "but he was a hell of a hypocrite about it and really played pious when he turned us in. So we figured he who tattles about booze shall also toss his booze."

Doctor Doyle reports that this additive will work easily with nonalcoholic drinks, too. He says the secret is to select a carrier drink that will hide the taste and consistency of the syrup.

Another good remedy for a hotshot is cascara sagrada, made from the dried root of a thorny shrub found on the American West Coast. It produces violent diarrhea. Once, Joe Kascaba introduced some cascara sagrada into a mark's orange juice. The mark was with his girlfriend and her parents in their family car. He had the "juiced" orange juice about ten minutes before getting into the car.

Kascaba reminisced, "The stuff's fast acting, and we were lucky to have the girlfriend's brother as our ally, to report the action. It hit the mark about six minutes into the trip, and in another minute he didn't even have time to yell for them to pull over. He just started letting go with loud, wet, explosive bursts.

"This is all in full witness of his girlfriend and her family in a tightly packed auto. He couldn't get stopped, either. They took him to a hospital, but by then the additive was through his system and the storm had subsided. That surely is super-powerful stuff."

Kascaba explained why he had taken this explosive action, saying, "The guy was a real creep. He was always trying to make out with other girls, and since he wasn't very smooth, he used to get them drunk. This was always with other girls, of course—his regular girlfriend knew nothing about all this.

"Well, one night he pulled this crap on a friend of mine, got her drunk, messed around . . . she got feeling all guilty and emotional, then got sick—puked, in fact. He thought he was macho stuff and gave her hell for it.

"We figured if he was going to act like such a shit . . . well, I'm sure you understand. . . ."

As a final note, Kascaba says not to use this powerful additive with older folks, because it may weaken them to the point of very serious medical consequences.

The following trick is technically a substitution and not an additive: I know of one person who visited her mark's home and emptied the hair conditioner out of its bottle, then poured Neet hair remover into the conditioner bottle. She knew that her Operation Substitute was a bald success when she saw her mark in a local store several weeks later, wearing a large scarf on her head.

Vinegar makes a great substitute for nose drops or in nasal-spray devices. One especially nasty person also suggested it for use in eye drops. I'm not sure about that one, though. Sight's a precious thing.

Airlines

Did an airline ever lose your luggage? Veteran air traveler Dottie Hunte suggests you return their favor and make yourself some money. Here's her scam. Arrange to have a friend meet you at the terminal gate when you deplane. Give your friend your baggage claim checks and have him/her retrieve your bags from the carousel, then leave the baggage area with your bags. Before your friend leaves the airport with the luggage, be sure you get your claim checks back. Then you saunter over to the baggage area and spend half an hour waiting for your bags. Ask some clerk for help, then report your "missing" luggage, showing your claim checks as proof.

"Very few flights ever have a clerk actually check the baggage and collect the claim checks," she says. "It's foolish, but they don't."

She suggests you "make a polite but firm scene and demand satisfaction. Normally, the airline people will have you fill out a form, and they will attempt to trace your luggage. Obviously, they won't find it. Bug them some . . . write them letters. Soon, you should get a good settlement from the airline." Don't pull this one on the same airline more than once, Hunte cautions.

Leaving the airlines and aiming for the individual mark, you can do a lot of personal damage. For instance, if you find that your mark is going to use airline travel and there are only a few travel agents in town, you could call until you find the correct one and cancel the reservations. Or if you know the name of the airline, call their office and cancel the mark's reservations.

You might try to slip a couple rounds of pistol ammunition or a switchblade knife into your mark's pocket just before he goes through the metal detector at the airport terminal. You could also slip some drugs into his pocket at the same time. Read a book on pickpocketing to note the technique for doing this. It's quite easy.

Bill Cutcheon sometimes poses as a Moonie, Hare Krishna devotee, or other cultist and goes to airports. His goal is to act a completely obnoxious fool. He really hams it up, usually getting tossed out after totally grossing out passengers. The heat, of course, falls equally on the cults and on the airport for letting "them" behave like that.

Another Cutcheon stunt is to leave accurate-looking but totally bogus hijack scenario plans, bomb diagrams, or orders of battle for terrorist attacks in airport bars and restrooms. This fires up both the rent-a-cops and the real security people. The security delays and resultant hassles with passengers create unhappy people who are angry at airports and airlines.

Naturally, the blame for these plans must focus on the original perpetrator of Cutcheon's problems. He says, "If some nut group's been hassling me for money, messing in my neighborhood, or otherwise being obnoxious, I'll leave evidence to pin the hijack or bomb rap on them. I got back at a motorcycle gang by doing this once, after they had sideswiped my truck and refused to pay damages."

He also explains that this is a good vengeance grabber against an airport facility that has offended you.

Mitch Egan of San Francisco doesn't like cultist panhandlers harassing people at airports, so he founded the Fellowship to Resist Organized Groups Involved in Exploitation, or FROGIE. Egan and his friends use those little metal clickers shaped like frogs to ward off religious solicitors.

According to Egan, thousands of people across the country are now armed with the little metal frogs, and when a religious panhandler approaches, they whip out the clicker and *"Click, click, click!"* the pest away.

"In San Francisco, I saw two hundred people clicking away at a Krishna," Egan remarked. "They blew her right out of her socks."

He adds, "If God wants a dollar from me, he can ask for it. I'm not against religion, but I'm fed up with organized beggars."

Relief is just a click away.

I knew a chap who became annoyed at a Krishna who followed him out of the Indianapolis airport, verbally abusing him for not making a contribution. Having surreptitiously "armed and primed" himself, our hero suddenly stopped, whipped around, and peed all over the startled harridan. After the few necessary seconds of attack, he calmly replaced himself, zipped up, and walked away. A bemused security cop standing nearby tried to hide his laughter.

Animals

If your mark is an oily cuss with a credibility problem, you could easily pull off this stunt suggested by good old country boy Emil Connally. It involves a cop, reporters, SPCA folk, and some farm animals.

According to Connally, here's how it works. You have two marks. The prime one is a farm owner with the credibility problem. We'll call him Mr. Big. The secondary mark is a cop who's made an enemy of you. In this case, pick one of your local Attila the Hun cops, because he's a bully and his ego for a bust will get in the way of his grain-sized brain.

Call the cop—try for his home phone even if it's unlisted—and tell him you know about a cock or dog fight that's being held at Mr. Big's farm. Explain you have no morals against animal fighting (build your own macho image) but you lost big money the last time and you think the fights are fixed. Mention drugs and booze, too. Next, call Mr. Big and tell him you're an anonymous political ally who wants to warn him about some people holding dog or cock fights at his farm. Call reporters and the SPCA and tell them all about the fight. Tell them that Mr. Big and the cop have a payoff relationship. Give everyone the same general arrival time . . . never be too specific.

If all goes well, all will sort of show up at roughly the same time. You might manipulate things so the press and animal lovers show up first. Even if a real story doesn't develop, you have scattered some stong seeds of distrust.

There is a variation if you want a stronger story. Kill and mutilate a dog or rooster, then bury it several days before you set up your animal-fight scenario at Mr. Big's place. Tell the reporters and the SPCA where the evidence is buried. It will be fun to hear the two marks talk about these things to the other parties. Maybe there's a story here after all.

Dead animals are so useful. Don't you agree? A nefarious lady known only as Hong Kong Hattie once waited until her mark went to the airport to depart for a five-day business trip. Then, using the nefarious methods for which she is so famous, Hattie got to the mark's car in the airport parking lot and got the lock opened. She then stuffed a large and very dead groundhog into the glove compartment. Hattie locked the car and strolled away. Reportedly, the mark sold his car at quite a financial loss just a few days after getting back from his business trip.

One of the plagues for newspaper deliverers is barking, biting dogs that attack both kids and their bicycles. Tom Frickert, today a newspaper magnate but once a paperboy, has a solution.

"A good-quality plastic water pistol filled with freshly squeezed lemon juice is the ticket," Frickert says with a chuckle. "You shoot the felonious furball right in the eyes, and it'll soon stop the canine harassment.

"I once shot a big, nasty cur with the juice, and he never bothered me again . . . used to hide under his master's porch whenever I came down the sidewalk to deliver the newspaper."

If your neighbor's constantly yowling and howling dog bothers you, congratulations, you're normal. But unlike most who sit and suffer, you can call the local SPCA and tell them how the neighbor mistreats the animal. Hold your phone near the window so the SPCA official can hear the "evidence" right from the source.

Apartments

Your mark lives in an apartment? A squirt or so of Eastman 910 or a similar type glue into the lock can screw up the mark's trying to get back into the apartment after an evening on the town. It's best to save this one until late evening or on a weekend. Of course, this same stunt would work on a house, but an apartment lockout disturbance creates more of a public scene.

If the mark's apartment is an older building with wooden door frames and you can work quietly and quickly at night, you can lock him/her in the apartment from the outside. Quietly fit a hasp and keeper on the door and frame using wood screws. Then slap a padlock on the new fixture. It creates a great deal of frustration if that door is the only way out of the apartment. Do it late Saturday night so the discovery is made on Sunday morning when it's impossible to get help.

Run a classified ad offering to sublet the mark's apartment. You can list either the mark's telephone number or that of his/her landlord. As usual, make the contact hour for very early in the morning "because of shift-work schedule."

You might want to make a "milk run" to the mark's apartment very early on several mornings and place a whole bunch of empty booze bottles outside his or her door. This works well in ritzy apartments where the neighbors are snobs. How do you get by the security people? One way is to pose as a delivery person, a service person, a building inspector, or someone on a work crew. You can also hire an accomplice in the building, or you can bribe the door guard.

Suppose you are the victim of a nasty landlord who evicts you for no good reason. There are lots of legal ways to get your tenant's rights, but there are also many quasi-legal and illegal ways that are much more fun. For example, you could simply "sublet" the place, on your own, to a bunch of dopers, bikers, drunks, hookers, runaways, or twenty-four-hour party throwers. Make this extracurricular subletting your going-away surprise.

Another person I know went to the local animal shelter on several different days and got a total of fifteen cats for twenty-five dollars. He bought a bunch of cat food and a bushel basket of fish, and filled his bathtub with water for them. He then nailed every window and door shut from the inside before crawling out the tiny casement window in the basement. He had previously nailed the basement door shut behind him. Obviously, he had moved his things out several days previously. His eviction notice was effective the next day, but the landlord didn't check on the house for five days. My God, what a mistake that man made. To say that that cat house was an uninhabitable mess is an understatement.

Tim Carroll was tossed out of his apartment by the landlady because one of Tim's many lady friends stayed over for the entire evening. This upset the old biddy who owned the building, and being a staunch, God-fearing charter member of the DAR, she canceled his lease and ordered him to leave the building.

Displeased with the arbitrary and unilateral treatment and the upheaval caused by her dubious moral judgment, Tim didn't get angry; he got even. He had a trusted friend place a large sign in a hallway window of the landlady's apartment building. The seventh-floor window faced a busy business street, and the sign was quite visible to many hundreds of people.

The sign read: TIM CARROLL SUCKS.

The landlady didn't see the sign, so two days later, Tim's friend positioned another sign, this time in a sixth-floor-hall window.

The second sign read: TIM CARROLL IS A FAG.

The landlady saw both signs and removed them. Two days later, she got a letter from Tim, with a picture enclosed showing her building with the signs easily visible. The letter was Tim's complaint about personal slander and harassment. He asked her please to desist.

Sometime early the next morning, in time for rush-hour morning traffic, a new sign went up in the window: TIM CARROLL BLOWS DEAD BEARS.

At 8:30 A.M., the unsuspecting landlady received a call from an attorney friend of Tim's, citing the original slander and warning the woman against further incidents. Shaken, she swore her innocence. Ten minutes after hanging up, he called back, sounding furious because Tim had just called him about the latest sign. Flabbergasted, the old lady swore she would remove it and loudly proclaimed her innocence.

Another sign went up that afternoon in time for rush hour the other way: TIM CARROLL IS A FLAMING HETEROSEXUAL.

The landlady got the lawyer's call just after dark, when the sign was no longer visible. She was almost in tears because of his threats to sue. She begged to just talk to Tim, to tell him none of this was her doing. The attorney told her that he had advised his client to have no further discussions with her.

The next day's sign read: FOR A GOOD LAY, CALL TIM CARROLL.

That evening, a new sign went up. The landlady, frantic, according to Tim's friend who was putting up the signs, got to it fifteen minutes after it went up. The attorney called her five minutes after she got back to her own apartment.

Tim related, "You might almost feel sorry for the old

lady, except that she had told me earlier that she was going to keep my security deposit and that I would have to forfeit the month's rent I had paid in advance because I had violated the morality clause in my lease. There was no such clause. I found out she had done this same thing to two other guys a year before and some guys before that. She also tossed out a couple because they weren't married. She'd come into your room when you were gone and snoop, too. That bugged me."

No signs went up for the next three days, although the woman checked the windows every twenty minutes or so. On the fourth day, hundreds of passersby, accustomed to the signs, weren't disappointed.

The new sign read: TIM CARROLL'S WHOREHOUSE.

Although it took her an hour to discover and remove it, the lawyer friend of Tim's didn't call until the next morning, when a new sign was in the window: WHOREHOUSE UNDER NEW MANAGEMENT. The landlady's telephone number was listed.

A second sign was placed in the sixth-floor window underneath: TIM CARROLL COULDN'T BEAT THE COMPETITION.

In his best tones, the attorney explained that enough was enough and that on behalf of his client, Mr. Carroll, he would be filing an action. The woman was distraught. He told her to have her attorney present for a meeting at three the following afternoon. He asked who her attorney was and said the meeting should be in his office. Tim and his attorney postponed this meeting several times, then told the woman that since she had stopped putting up the signs, they would hold the suit in limbo for the time.

Reportedly, she monitored the halls and windows of that building regularly for five months. But more importantly, she also left her tenants to their own moral lives.

April First

Just as professional drinkers retire from the field of play on New Year's Eve, allowing the turf to be chewed up by dumbass amateurs, skilled operators in the dirty-tricks business leave April First to the KICK ME-sign-on-the-pants crowd.

Assassination

Suppose you have a mark whose ill temper has created problems for you. Or perhaps this mark is simply an obnoxious nut whose obsessions have cost you personally. A dentist I know spent many unselfish hours working to get fluoride into his community's drinking water as a means of fighting tooth decay in children. An apolitical and highly dedicated professional, he was concerned only with health care for the kids in the community. A hyper, rightwing zealot jumped on the issue and scared the town council with his insane babble. He claimed that fluoride was a Communist plot to poison America's water and minds and that using fluoride would lead to LSD as part of the International Communist Conspiracy. The timid council voted "no" on fluoride.

Beside himself, the young dentist said he surely would like to get back at that rightwing firebrand but just didn't know what to do. Sighing, he gave up his fight and put his time back into his practice. The kids never got their fluoride treatment, and as a result he had a lot of business. It's too bad that young dentist never met Maurice Bishop.

In the hypocritical piety following the assassinations of the sixties, physical security was supposedly tightened to protect the chief executive chosen by the power brokers who now control the United States. A former law-enforcement official with a probable intelligence background offered an astounding dirty trick related to this topic. To protect this source's identity we'll use the cover name of Maurice Bishop.

Bishop says the CIA, FBI, and Secret Service all keep a list of nut cases, radicals, and others who threaten political figures. Often, these people are jailed, kept under protective custody, or placed under twenty-four-hour surveillance by authorities when political targets are in the area. Bishop's idea calls for threatening telegrams to be sent to the politician in the mark's name. At the very least this telegram will bring a visit by one of the government agencies, and perhaps it will result in a bit of jail time if the mark loses his/her cool as a result of this dirty trick.

Bishop says this will also work with state officials, bringing a visit from state police or some other law-enforcement official.

Auto Dealers

If an automobile dealership screws you, on either the car, the deal, or the service, don't get angry—get even. Wait outside the showroom until a prospective customer starts talking to a salesperson about the same type of car you got. Walk right up to the customer and tell your woeful story. The idea is to screw up as many sales as you can. Be factual, be cool, and act as if you're an honest citizen trying to save another honest citizen some money and heartache—as you wish someone had done for you. Sincere good faith is the thing here, because the salesman is going to blow his about the second time you pull your act.

When the manager asks you to leave and you don't, he will probably call the police. You had anticipated this earlier and alerted someone at the local newspaper or television station—probably the action-line reporters. Smalltown media usually won't allow reporters to come— car dealers buy lots of ads, and you don't. A regional TV station may show up—if you promise a confrontation with the law. So when the manager calls the police, you call your TV reporter—fun and games for the 6:00 P.M. news.

If all this doesn't work, wait off the dealer's premises and approach customers as they leave the showroom. Tell your story there and then. Offer to help them avoid your mistake. But stay on public property. And keep after the action-line reporters.

If you want to escalate the attack a bit, show up when the night salespeople are on duty—they won't recognize you. Look at new cars; wander around. Few salespeople pay much attention to an obvious gawker. As soon as someone else or a telephone distracts the salesperson, you can do things to the automobile right there in the showroom. A bottle opener is hard on the finish. See the section on additives for things you could quickly put into the fuel tank. If you could smuggle some in with you, stuff roadkill under a car seat or in the glove compartment. Or toss a condom (preferably used) on the front seat. By the way, used condoms make wonderful plants in other locations as well, like the boss's desk, or in a customer's car back in the service shop.

If you can manage to slip undetected into the service area along with your bag of sabotage goodies, such as glue, wire cutters, paint, potatoes, M80s, etc., you can run amok. Work quietly and quickly. This sort of guerrilla warfare can literally wreck a dealer's service reputation.

Banks

It could be time to make your bankroll. According to Townsend Alexander, our financial intelligence agent, you can make good money buying some very cheap foreign coins that are the same size as quarters. Get a paper coin wrapper. Wrap a few real quarters on the ends but fill the rest of the roll with the cheapie import coins. Wrap the roll and with felt-tip pen write some phony account number on it to add authenticity.

Take the rolls of coins into the targeted bank. If you dress like a businessperson and go at a busy time, especially with the account number written on each roll, and the rolls in a bank sack or your briefcase, the teller will probably give you ten dollars per roll without checking.

If you could get a banker to tell the truth, he'd admit that they hate college-student checking accounts. There's probably a lot of justification, since most services like this for college students cost far more than they're worth in return. However, that's not our problem.

Suppose you have a gripe with the bank. Acting as the bank's ad manager, get in touch with the student newspaper at the school and arrange to run some ads with banner headlines reading, STUDENTS WELCOME, plus such services as NO SERVICE CHARGE, FREE CUSTOM-PRINTED CHECKS, INTEREST ON THE BALANCE, NO MINIMUM BALANCE, and so on. Offer to give away free albums or transistor radios. The day after the "bank's" ad runs they will be swamped with unwanted students, who are going to be very angry at the bank (and probably at the student newspaper).

Modern banks now have cash machines where you insert your plastic card and the machine gives you money. If that institution or its machine has become your target, here's a dairyland delight you could employ. Take some tough, hard cheese and cut it the same size and shape as your plastic card. Insert the cheese "card" into the slot of the machine and leave the area. One banker told me it took a service person nine hours to clean the machine and get it operating again when someone pulled this stunt in Baltimore.

The bank still giving you trouble, or you didn't give them enough? It's time to move things up the scale a notch. Rent a safe-deposit box under another name. Pay cash for a three-month rental. That's all the time you'll need to collect on this one. Go to the market and buy a couple of overripe fish—I'm sure you'll get a bargain price. Carry them wrapped in plastic in your briefcase. Go directly to your safe-deposit box. In the privacy of the bank's little cubicle, unwrap the fish and lay the big, stinky suckers right in the safe-deposit box. Close it, lock it, and store it. Then carry the fish wrappers, briefcase, and yourself out of that bank. In a few days your deposit will gain their interest. You'd better do your real banking at another institution for a while. It's quite possible bank officials will have to hire someone to drill the lock on the targeted safe-deposit box to remove the contents.

Bikers

You're walking along a pedestrian sidewalk, and along comes a bicyclist, churning away his/her spare calories on that nonpolluting transportation device. Within moments you're an involuntary participant in a game of chicken with that cyclist, who swerves while you weave. You finally pass each other in good dodgeum-car fashion. Maybe. Wonderful stuff, adrenaline.

On the other cheek, maybe you've been blindsided by an irresponsible cyclist trespassing on your pedestrian-walk right of way.

"No more turning the other cheek," is the war cry of Mel Scafe, an anticyclist who is fighting back.

"I've declared war on all two wheelers who trespass into my life," Mel says. "I'll get the senior citizen bicyclist who forces me off my sidewalk on the same day I get even with the teenage dirt biker who tears up the hill behind my home."

One of Mel's tactics is to toss a length of chain into the spokes of the dirt bike when it's roaring by. Instantly, the bike stops going forward while the rider continues onward until gravity takes over.

"I've also used a wire cutter to snip the spokes on a bicycle whose owner has done me a disfavor," Mel relates. "That'll cause a real collapse in his biking game."

Another time he spread a large patch of grease on the

path used by dirt bikers.

He can't even estimate the pounds of air he's released from captivity in bike tires. He's used all the nasty engine additives mentioned earlier in this book for these machines that disturb his world.

"I liked that Burt Reynolds movie where the truck driver drove his rig over all those goddamn motorcycles," Mel grinned. Turning serious, he added, "I've thought about the old World War II trick of stretching piano or barbed wire across a trail or bikeway, but I think that could be fatal, so I don't really do it.

"If there were some way I could totally kill the damn machines and only embarrass the people a bit I'd surely like to hear about it. Until then I will stick to the old standards that have worked for me so far."

He adds, "I know people may sneer at me for being mean to kiddies on their bicycles, and I know bicycles are an in thing today. But maybe if those young riders learn some manners early and stay the hell off pedestrian walks, they might grow up to be decent people."

Books

Did anyone ever borrow a book from you and not return it? Our private library consultant, Roberta Russell, has a suggestion with an air of financial finality behind it. For the first step, a printer should make you about three or four dozen bookplates, all featuring your mark's name and address, plus the legend, "If this book is lost and you find it and return it, I will pay you $10 cash." Your next step is the local Goodwill Industries, a local thrift or second-hand shop, or a garage sale for books. Buy two or three dozen used hardcover books. You buy them as cheaply as you can, but they'll cost your mark plenty. Your next step is to paste on the bookplates and distribute these books—at the beach, on park benches, in a bus or subway, or in a bar or restaurant. The final step is for you to enjoy a good chuckle at your mark's expense, as people find the "lost" books.

If your mark has a fine library, you might consider introducing it to silverfish. They love good books; in fact, they will devour them. If you really feel this nasty, you probably already know where to get silverfish and their eggs. This one bothers me, though, since I love good books. Maybe there's a better way. Perhaps you could put an earwig in your mark's bed pillow.

Why not give your mark the image of a philanthropic person? Donate books in his/her name to the local library, but without either party's knowledge. Buy a bunch of really scuzzy porno paperbacks, especially the colorfully illustrated ones from Denmark—the more grossly hardcore, the better. Your printer will produce some paste-in bookplates that say something like, "This book donated to the [Name] library by [Mark's Name] in loving memory of all the sweet children of [Town Name]." Paste in the bookplates and sprinkle the donated books around the local library. Put some in the children's section, and others in with the religion books.

Campuses

Not everyone is hibernating on college campuses. Although it's true that many students have become docile zombies, lobotomized by lethal doses of television and the bureaucracy of the educational system, there arc a few live ones. At an eastern university, a number of students got upset with the rent gouging of a massive corporation acting as an absentee landlord for private off-campus dormitories. After getting nowhere appealing to an untesticled school administration, and after being ignored by a housing inspector and a city council belonging to the same social class and clubs as the corporate landlords, the students held a pizza party.

The unusual part was that the pizza party was held in the clothes dryers of the dormitory laundry rooms. One participant reported, "We dumped a couple of really gooey pizzas in each dryer, put in the coins, and turned them on."

Try cleaning up that one!

Epilogue: The corporate landlord and his student tenants settled their problems shortly after the party, totally to the satisfaction of the young protestors.

Professor James Shannon claims that college students of the past had heinous imaginations. Today, of course, many students are content merely to move around enough to prevent roots from forming on their contact surfaces with the ground. Professor Shannon suggests that if you have a teacher you don't like, and he/she lectures from a desk or podium on a raised platform, you move the stand so its legs are barely balanced on the front edge of the platform. When the academic leans forward on the structure ever so slightly, it will come crashing forward. With any luck the pedagogue will land on top of it.

At an eastern university, two looser colleagues filled a humorless and bookish faculty member's office closet with several very large and irritable geese late one evening. The professor was in the habit of arriving quite early for his 8:00 A.M. class, early enough so that the hasty-tempered birds would just be awakening. When he opened the closet door they woke up and became badly aggressive really fast. Eyewitness reports left no doubt whose feathers were ruffled most.

This will be truly appreciated only by those privy to the pettiness of academia: Other colleagues of this same professor sometimes send truly pedantic, nasty, personal, and vindictive memoranda to various other faculty members, deans, etc., in the name of their priggish colleague.

On one occasion they sent really nasty letters to the parents of a few of this faculty member's students, giving the poor folks hell for daring to produce such genetic drift as their kids, much less turning them loose on a college campus. The school's PR people had a terrible time getting out from under that one. As for the mark, the dumb schmuck had no idea why so many people disliked him. But please take his colleagues' word for it—he deserves every bit of it.

Carbide

Having been brought up around hunters and miners, I learned all about carbide lamps and carbide fishing early. Working on my grandfather's farm, I learned about carbide bombs. Let me explain some things you might find useful.

When calcium carbide is exposed to air and water it produces a gas that will kill small animals. Farmers often pour it down gopher, rat, or groundhog holes, then dump in some water and put a rock over the hole. The animal is gassed to death.

A lot of poor people used to fish with carbide with the same efficiency with which legions of GIs fished with hand grenades. Simply toss a pound or two of carbide into a can and seal it, but be sure to punch a few holes in the lid. Toss it into a pond. The results can play havoc with your mark's fish pond or fancy goldfish pool or an indoor aquarium. Water and carbide can produce an explosion.

Some of the nastier kids used to place amounts of carbide into the toilets at our school. The idea was to place the carbide bomb in the toilet, leave a lighted cigarette on the seat, and run like hell. The carbide would combine with the water to produce a huge cloud of noxious gas, which would explode when it hit the lighted cigarette the perpetrators left behind. This little homemade bomb did more damage than an M80.

Tim Bell, who later became a Special Forces NCO in

Vietnam, explains, "We had this kid bully whom no one liked—a real prick. He always went to the john after fourth period to sneak a smoke. So two of us went in right after him and laid a carbide bomb in the water in the next stall. We were about a hundred feet down the hall when the damn thing went off."

At this point, Tim burst into wild laughter. I was able to learn, though, that the bully had his legs burned and cut by flying porcelain, bit his tongue badly, was knocked violently off the throne, bruising his ribs against the steel wall of the stall, and was deafened for nearly twenty-four hours, all by the force of this carbide explosion. With that kind of background as a high school kid, it's no wonder Tim Bell made a good Special Forces trooper.

Are there more adult uses for carbide? Some sixties semi-terrorists used to dump a pound or so into the toilets of corporate offices and government buildings, flush the mess into the system, and walk away briskly. Enough of the stuff could get very dangerous, considering the possible backup of gases. A combination of water and carbide has been fed into the ventilating systems of various corporate and government buildings, also by semi-terrorists who wish to harass the resident bureaucrats.

Cars

This one's really kiddie Halloween time, but it does work. A bunch of old nuts and bolts placed into the wheel well behind the hubcap will make the mark think his/her car is falling apart. It's worth some minor harassment, of course, and works outstandingly well with high-strung nonmechanical types who absolutely panic at car noises.

You can get a little heavier than Halloween by removing a hubcap from your mark's car wheel and loosening or removing the lug bolts. Sooner or not much later, the wheel will simply roll off the car.

Moving up the escalator of nastiness, you could probably fill your mark's whole body with adrenaline if you placed a split shot sinker, of the type used by fishermen, on the accelerator cable of his/her vehicle. Willy Seamore, a top mechanic, suggests you extend the cable, then place the lead weight on the extended portion, which effectively blocks it from returning. This means the vehicle's throttle will run wide open. It's a nasty version of the jack-rabbit start.

From choking up to locking up is hardly a quantum experience. The new miracle glues are impregnable when squirted into car door keyholes. Nothing short of a locksmith can repair this low-risk attack. If you hit just before the mark's family vacation, leave the car door locks alone and hit the trunk lock. With any luck, they'll never notice until they're miles from home.

A refinement of simply putting a super glue or epoxy in the car's various locks is to take any old key that will vaguely fit into the lock cavity, insert it, then twist it rapidly back and forth until the key breaks off, stuck in the lock. Now is the time to squirt the glue into the lock. The job is more permanent and more costly to repair.

If you tire of fooling with the locks, you can look elsewhere. Marshall Tanner, inventor of muffler bearings, says you can prop some large-headed nails against the tires of your mark's car, especially if it's parked so it will have to be backed up to get out of a parking stall in a lot. The car moves back and the wheels roll over the nails, puncturing tires.

If your mark's married, you can have all sorts of sport with his ride. A male mark deserves that you slip sexy undergarments usually worn by a sexy lady under his car's front seat or wedge them carefully into the back seat. You could tear them a bit. More than a hint of perfume or flavored douche will always hype suspicion. You can escalate this stunt somewhat if you buy male underwear— get the sexy style in white—and place some lipstick smears around the fly area. You can help the campaign along by having a very trusted lady friend call and ask nervously for the mark. The younger she sounds, the better. Have her call several times. Use your and the mark's wife's imagination.

If the mark is a woman, a pack of condoms carelessly hidden in the car is always a sure-grow plant. Several dainty handkerchiefs of the type favored by milady and heavily impregnated with semen can also be stuffed in the car. As with the male, a series of appropriately timed telephone calls from a nervous male will add to the marital festivities between mark and spouse.

In less carnal surroundings, If you can get to the distributor cap, remove it and use graphite from a pencil to contact the rotor brushes. The charge will run along the graphite, causing the engine to misfire. This could cause the mark to dash into his local car butcher and get charged an outrageous price for an unnecessary tuneup.

A quick way to disable a car battery is to slip a couple of Alka-Seltzer tablets or a teaspoonful of baking soda into each battery compartment. The antacid will kill the battery's power before you can say "Plop, plop, fizz, fizz."

Another camhead nasty is to take a pushpin and jab a few tiny holes through spark-plug wires. According to Lee H. Santana, a real straight shooter in the dirty-tricks department, the pin pricks cause a hellishly rumpety noise when the car is driven.

Don't forget additives when working on a mark's car. The nice thing about additives is that you don't have to be odd or even to use them. Many experts, including some of Uncle Sam's khaki-clad nephews, suggest light materials, such as crushed cork, as a great additive to the gasoline tanks of vehicles belonging to people or institutions you don't like.

One former professional trickster said, "It isn't exotic, but a handful of old leaves in the gas tank will bind the damn engine up too."

Sand is not recommended because of its weight, especially when wet. It would sink to the bottom of the tank and not much would be introduced into the engine, he explained. The idea is to get the additive to the bearing surfaces, where the coarse little buggers can kick and scratch up a mechanical breakdown. Silicone carbide, emery powder, and fine metal filings will work. During World War II, our OSS used a mixture of finely ground cork, resins, carborundums, and metal alloys to muck up an engine.

Another method that could possibly send a driver off to a service station would be to pour a gallon of shellac thinner into your targeted vehicle's gasoline tank. The alcohol will gather up all the water in the fuel trap, and when this mixture goes through the fuel line it will cause the vehicle to snort, stammer, and act as if it has big carb troubles. By the time the driver gets the vehicle to a mechanic, the problem has usually departed out the exhaust pipe. Done enough times, this one can redline the frustration and credibility levels of both the driver and the mechanic.

If you want to use additives in your mark's gasoline tank, yet are concerned about arousing suspicion in daylight or in an otherwise high-visibility area, simply adopt a cover prop.

"Put the harmful additive in a metal gasoline can like they sell in stores," advises Joey MacJohns, a veteran trickster. "That way, any potential witnesses will never really pay attention to what's happening; they'll simply infer because you have a gas can that you're putting gas in the car."

And don't forget *oil* additives. Styrene, a colorless, oily liquid, is an organic compound that is one of the two chemicals mixed together to make hardened fiberglass. Boat-supply stores and marinas have styrene available for patching fiberglass boats. It is also used in body shops and upholstery-repair places.

There are substitute compounds that will do the same job as styrene, so read the label when purchasing the stuff to make sure you're actually getting styrene. Styrene is the only sufficiently effective, commonly available material that can be put into a car's crankcase to completely break down the oil and ruin the engine.

Styrene in the crankcase is far better than sugar in the gas tank because it can't be seen after being introduced and because only a little does a thorough job. If it's used at the rate of one pint per four quarts of oil, the treated vehicle will run about a hundred miles before the engine locks up tight.

This is a fairly high-risk stunt, but it could be fun if you don't get nailed doing it, according to Bill Rally. If you find that your mark is going alone to a movie you have an hour or so to have some fun with his automobile. If you're motivated enough to carry off this stunt, no one has to tell you how to start the mark's car without a key. After you start it, drive to some very nice homes with pretty lawns. But stay fairly near the theater, so you can get back there in a hurry. Do donuts, dig out, and otherwise use the car to make a shambles of lawns, shrubbery, flower beds, etc. Run over lawn furniture, hit mailboxes, and try to frighten some old people by coming really close to them with the car.

This is a real hit-and-run mission. Do your dirty driving fast and get the car back to the theater parking area even faster. Park it and leave. If you've done enough damage, all sorts of police reports will be out on the car. The second or third question the police will ask the mark is whether he or she has any witnesses for the movie alibi.

That can be a real blast. But if you want another sort of pop, dig deeply into the potato bin for this one. My thanks here go to all those great truck farmers who say a potato jammed into a vehicle's exhaust pipe is not explosive, but it will cause all sorts of nasty problems. In one case, the mark parked his car with the rear end toward his home. His tormentor jammed a fresh, hard spud tightly into the car's exhaust pipe. The mark started the car on a cold evening and waited a few moments for the engine to warm. Meanwhile, the hot gases, unable to escape, built up dangerously behind the potato. . . . *Woom!* . . . *KABLOOM!* . . . With an explosive roar, the gases fired that big, hot, hard potato right into the metal siding of the mark's home, just fifteen feet away from the exhaust pipe, which had acted as a cannon barrel. The holing and denting of the siding cost $150 and a day to repair.

There are all sorts of other devices that make good muffler bombs. A firecracker may be shoved into the vehicle's exhaust pipe, pushing it along with a stiff wire until the explosive device falls into the muffler. It takes only a few moments of driving with today's hot exhaust gases to explode the firecracker. Even a fairly small firecracker will cause panic, especially if the driver is paranoid to start with. If you want to destroy the muffler and drive the mark's panic into the fantasy of having his/her car really bombed, substitute an M80 or a shotgun shell for the prankish finger-sized firecracker.

If the violence and property destruction of this bothers you or causes you to grimace, consider this next happy face. Most mail-order and novelty stores sell very realistic rubber face masks, resembling everything from an ape man, through a drooling idiot, on down to a Ronald Reagan mask. Select one that looks especially gross—like an old man, or the idiot, or Richard Nixon. Position it so it looks realistic on the back of your head. This leaves your vision unobstructed. Head for the road in your car.

Just as another motorist overtakes your vehicle to pass you, lean out the window. The effect on the approaching motorist would be interesting to observe, as that other driver will see a drooling goon looking back, directly at him, with no apparent concern for the road ahead. I bet very few cars actually pass you with this stunt in operation.

Taking the license plate off a mark's car can be a good shot, even you don't want to steal the thing for other nefarious purposes. How many times do you look to see if the plate is on your car? A cop has to look only once. I bet it would be fun to hear the mark's explanation of where his license plate has gone.

Don't you get really happy when some defective excuse for a human suddenly pulls his/her vehicle out directly in front of yours or cuts you off? Marty Mullin has a solution in hand.

A delightful person, Mullin reveals, "I bought a top-quality pellet pistol, one of those compressed-air guns, which I keep in my car. You can use either the cartridge or the pump type—just be sure you get one with enough power to penetrate metal. Get a supply of the .177-caliber pellets, too. Then, next time some dip pulls out in front of you, pull up behind the dip's vehicle and get in his/her blind spot. With a truck or van that's easy enough. Then you bring your pellet gun into action.

"Plunk a shot into the mark's vehicle, the trunk for a car, or the back of a van or rig. If it's a big truck you can get in quite a few shots, because the driver is not likely to hear them. A van or car will make a helluva *twhunk* when that pellet hits, so be cautious.

"There's no discharge noise, because you're not using a firearm. After your attack, back off and proceed about your business as if nothing has happened. You probably have not taught the mark a lesson, but you'll feel better for what you just did—I guarantee that."

I asked Mullin about the possibility of hitting a passenger who is riding in the back of the mark's vehicle. He replied, "Then, that passenger also has every right to be furious with the dippy mark for pulling out in front of you."

Charities

Charity begins at the home of your mark. You simply volunteer his/her services to the charity's recruiting chairperson, giving the name and address of the mark. These charity drives are so happy to get volunteers these days that they will rarely verify your call. That means the first contact the mark has is when another volunteer shows up at the door with all sorts of campaign and collection materials. In many cases, the mark is too embarrassed to refuse, and you've added to his/her workload.

If you think that's a dirty trick to pull on a charity, ask them how many cents out of each dollar go directly to the victims and other people who are at the bottom of the line for help. Besides, your mark might turn out to be a great charity worker.

You can call in generous pledges in your mark's name during telethons and other charity drives.

You can also call in pledges to bothersome telethons, using double-entendre names. For example, when one public-TV station held another of its semiweekly fundraisers, several contributors announced over the air as pledging financial support included Clint Toris, Seymour Kunt, Connie Lingus.

Margie Kowalski used to work for the Salvation Army. She suggests that you call the local Salvation Army,

Goodwill, or whatever charity and report your mark for stealing out of the organization's pickup boxes. Report the mark by his auto license number. Say you work at one of the stores near the collection box and you've seen the mark rob the box several times. You can also report this "crime" to the police.

Cheese

It's tried and true, but I bet you haven't heard of it since you were a kid. This one came from Alabama, the old Limburger-cheese-on-the-muffler-of-a-new-car trick. The exhaust manifold works well, too, as a surface for a cheese spread. Or you can simply place some of the same substance behind a radiator in a home or office. Once it's burned on, the smelly sour effect can last for weeks, despite robust cleaning efforts.

Child Abuse

I heard a real horror story recently where a truly evilminded teenager swore to child-abuse officers in her county that her parents beat her. They hadn't and didn't. Never mind; the bureaucrats came bouncing out of the woodwork, and the harried parents had to appear in court to defend themselves against the lies of a teenager with mental problems. The parents were looked upon as villains, even though the judge dismissed the charges as unfounded. Their attorney (yes, they had to hire one to fight government persecution) advised them against a jury trial because they'd lose on the emotionalism of the issue, regardless of the facts. Nice.

All this leads up to the fact that you can report your mark as a child-abuse offender. Acting as a "concerned neighbor," you can tell the authorities. The hassle is unreal. After you've done this, a few anonymous letters to the mark's employer about the "child-abuse thing" will help out.

CIA

Your mark might have sneaky points you never thought about. For example, maybe your mark would make a good CIA employee. You could easily find out. Write a letter of application to the agency using your mark's name. The agency gets hundreds of letters from would-be action agents, such as unemployed gangsters, karate freaks, ex-soldiers, Walter Mitty types, etc. I doubt that they take many of these seriously, but they might be interested in talking with a highly qualified technical person, such as an analyst, area expert, journalist with oodles of foreign experience, language expert, or economist. Advanced college degrees and military service abroad as an officer are fine credentials for your mark. Make up a good solid background. It is probably illegal for you to make a false application in your mark's name using phony credentials.

Send resumes to:

Personnel Representative
Central Intelligence Agency
Washington, D.C. 20505

You can also send in an application in your mark's name for a CIA job at the field office in the nearest city. Yes, they are listed in the telephone book.

CB Radio

Want to send your neighborhood CB nut a message? This nut is the CB addict who refuses to filter his/her equipment and thus disrupts TV, stereo, AM/FM, and other normal communication for blocks. Usually, these idiots are about as sensitive to other people's feelings as Idi Amin was to the plight of the poor. In both cases a lesson is called for.

To do this effectively, heed the lesson of Sterling Orco, who says you must personally interdict the mark's CB antenna. It would be well to do this when the mark is away from the home area. Unfasten the CB coax line from the mark's antenna. Then clip two leads of a regular 110-volt line to the CB coax—one lead to the center conductor, the other lead to the shield. Small alligator clips will do nicely. Then, hop down from your perch near the antenna and plug the other end of the 110-volt wire into your mark's nearest outdoor socket.

Next time he/she turns on the CB and hits the transmit button . . . well, words fail to describe the results adequately. One comment—even the repair people will shake their heads.

A bit less destructive, but no less nasty, is the old pin-in-the-coax trick. You prick a tiny pin through the plastic outer cable and through the shield. Be sure it touches the center conductor. Then cut the head off the pin and push it in some more—out of sight. The plastic should close behind the pin, making the wound invisible. Just make sure that the pin short-circuits the center conductor to the metal outer shield. Do a couple of these along the coax between the antenna and the CB set. It does stuttering wonders for the transmission.

Classified Ads

Classified advertisements in your local newspaper are inexpensive little bullets that can cause major wounds to the mark's psyche if properly aimed. For instance, suppose you had a score to settle with some bitchy neighbors. You could insert a classified ad to "sell" their automobile. Price it five hundred dollars less than market value, instruct callers to call after midnight (shift work is the explanation you can offer), and explain in the ad that quick cash is needed for an emergency. That will bring in the phone calls.

You can also put your mark's house up for sale. Again, ask potential customers to either call or visit at hours that will be very inconvenient to the mark.

The "personals" in newspapers can provide even more fun. Maybe your mark ought to advertise for "young boy and girl models to pose for 'art' pictures." You should use his/her home or business telephone here for return calls, whichever would cause more difficulty for the mark.

Placing ads is a snap. Most newspapers let you do it right over the phone, and most of the ad people I've talked to say they rarely verify a classified ad. Take a tip from that and don't make it outlandish. As with any practical joke, there has to be a credible amount of reality to the premise for the sting to work.

While you're thinking of newspapers, don't forget those sexy tabloids and their really gross cousins that let readers advertise all sorts of weird sex things. I don't know whether any of that is on the level, but it's worth finding out—in your mark's name, of course. Maybe you'll be doing him/her a favor. But somehow I doubt it—there's no such thing as a free lunch.

You might help the mark share his new friends' sexual talents. Place an ad in one of the target audience magazines—the publication that runs very explicit and very honest classifieds. If you're not sure, contact a local sympathizer and ask him/her for help.

You might write your ad copy like this:

"Soft white male aged 35 wants to play with black lady with large buttocks. Bi-couples welcomed for Greek and French culture."

You can make bondage and S/M optional, depending upon reality, the publication, its audience, and your mark. You really ought to study the target publication before you word the ad. The kicker is that you will register the mark as sponsor of the classified ad. Read the section of this book that tells about using a neighbor's address and the mark's name before you get started.

If you do decide to run kinky classified ads for your mark in *Screw, Ball*, and whatever, be sure you get some copies of the issue in which the ad runs. That way you can send originals or Xerox copies to the mark's neighbors, relatives, business associates, and friends. Enclose a brief note asking how they can even admit knowing such a perverted person. Offer to pray for them. You could use the name and address of another friend, neighbor, or business associate as the return address for this note.

Help your mark out of the closet by running a classified announcement ad in homosexual publications. Have her/him grandly and proudly announce that he or she is gay and has dated and/or married only for cover. Now, he/she is coming out and telling the world she/he has taken a lover—and name a friend, neighbor, or business associate as that lover. Libelous? Yes, it is. Don't get caught.

Using classified advertising, Bill Colbeley had an auction for one of his many marks. He followed the usual auction format to prepare the newspaper ad, then ran it when the mark and his family were away for a weekend. The ad was one of those "Job transfer—everything must go—fantastic bargains" types so normal to an industrial community. But let Sweet Old Bill tell the rest of his story:

"I set the time of the auction for 7:00 A.M., so that just as the sleepy mark was rolling out of the sack about that hour, he looks out on his yard and sees about three hundred salesgoers uot there trampling all over his lawn, garden, and flowers. It took an hour for the mark and the police he called to get the crowd out of there."

Although it's not strictly a classified advertisement, the little index-card notices that people place on bulletin boards in bars, supermarkets, laundromats, and other public places are great ways to harass your mark. Just about anything you can use in a newspaper can be used on these more personal notices. But the advantages are, they don't cost anything but the time required to prepare and post them, and you can be a lot more wordy, descriptive, and personal than you can with a newspaper advertisement. Folks seem to read these very regularly too, as I know from my personal use of this community advertising medium with legitimate messages.

Clergy

One of the most useful bits of armament in the trickster's arsenal is a set of clerical garb. Lenny Bruce proved how financially useful this disguise is when he panhandled Miami dressed in a religious costume. But then, organized religion has known this for years, profitably practicing their old proverb "Let us prey."

Obtain and make use of overt religious garb. It creates a wonderfully secure and trustworthy image. Drug marketeers often use priest and nun outfits when moving dope. In Ireland, weapons and explosives are smuggled by kindly-looking middle-aged persons disguised as religious figures.

Your possibilities are limitless.

Coins

If consumer attorney Dale Richards is correct, more Americans lose money to coin-operated vending machines than lose money gambling or paying taxes to the IRS. What's also astounding is that so few people rise above simple vandalism as a response.

Richards explains, "Many vending companies are quite liberal in their refund policy. They don't question most refund requests. However, getting refunds is annoying to people, it takes time, and the machines shouldn't cheat people in the first place."

People who work for vending companies claim that customer vandalism is why the machines don't work in the first place. Critics claim that vandalism-repair cost is built into the price for the goods and services you get from coin machines. I'm not here to adjudicate this debate, but to pass along some alternative philosophy.

Abbie Hoffman says that every time you drop a coin down the slot of some vending machine you are losing money needlessly. There are many inexpensive foreign coins that will duplicate the American version and operate vending equipment. It may be tough to get some of these coins, because many legitimate dealers look suspiciously upon attempted purchases of large numbers of cheapie foreign coins. You could tell them that you use them for jewelry. Apparently, many coin dealers are establishment snitches, so be careful.

Here, according to Hoffman, are some of the more useful foreign coins. The Icelandic five-auran piece is the most effective substitute for an American quarter. They are hard to come by, since they are no longer minted. The Uruguayan ten-centisimo coin will also substitute for the U.S. quarter in a variety of vending machines, parking meters, telephones, toll gates, laundromats, etc. It does not work in cigarette machines. The Danish five-ore piece works in just about anything but pop and cigarette machines.

Dime-sized coins include the Malaysian penny, which works in a wide variety of machines and devices that take a dime. Some of the newer vending machines will reject this dime substitute. Another ersatz dime is the Trinidad penny.

You might be able to have friends who travel abroad get you rolls of these coins for collection purposes or to make jewelry.

Computers

The computer won't really be human until it can make a mistake, then cover up by blaming the error on some other hapless machine. More than one critic has pointed out that it is machines, not people, that both run and ruin our society. It seems perfectly proper, then, to seek vengeance against these tyrannical mechanical masters of ours. Most of us have the advantage when fighting a machine, because we can reason, we can note shades of gray, and we can think abstractly, beyond a set program. Machines cannot do this, unless some person translates these abstract notions into programmed sets of yes or no.

The classic way of fighting a computer is to punch a few extra holes in the computer card. This, of course, screws up the system, and the computer regurgitates your card. A supervisor must handle the situation manually, which costs money and time. People punch these extra holes in cards using a keypunch machine at a nearby school, or they simply and carefully cut a keypunch pattern with an X-acto art knife.

This sticky trick delights repair people, in addition to you. Place a large strip of Scotch tape on several computer cards. The slippery surface causes cards to fall off the track and into the bowels of the machine. A repair person has to come and perform mechanical surgery on the machine to remove your fatal paper bullets that felled the machine. This sort of dirty trick can tie up equipment for several hours of very, very costly down time.

Should the opportunity arise that you have a few secure moments with some reels of computer tapes and you want to screw up whoever or whatever controls the data on these tapes, you might try passing a portable electromagnet back and forth across the tapes. It erases them just the way a bulk eraser cleans off your audio tapes at home. In many cases computer-tape records are the only records kept by companies and schools.

Contractors

Just suppose your new home wasn't quite what the contractor ordered and promised. If you're lucky, you'll discover this sad fact before he's done working on the house. If not, you'll have to chase him to his next job site. I once went through that many years ago, and it can be fun.

Anyway, here's what you do. Erect a huge sign on your lot that says something like, BUY THIS UNDER-CONSTRUCTED, POORLY DONE HOME—CHEAP. Display the contractor's name and telephone number prominently. When he complains, tell him you wouldn't think of subjecting your family to the horrors of living in such a poorly constructed dump, and if he buys it you'll take down the sign. Have a list of things you think are wrong with the house. You have already shown him your list if you had to eventually resort to the big sign. Show him again. The heading of the list should state his name, address, and telephone number along with your general beef about the poor quality of his work, followed by the specific complaints. Mimeograph this list so your contractor will think you're handing them out faster than a politician's calling card. It's worked well in the past. You should get your grievances satisfied.

A man calling himself Hank suggested one for the construction trade. He says that if your mark is building anything from concrete and you or your allies have access to that concrete before it is poured, add concentrated hydrochloric acid to it. Hank claims, "I've seen it work—it causes slow but continual deterioration of the structure from corrosion."

Credit Cards

Designed as a credit convenience for consumers and a big profit turner for business, credit cards are impersonal pieces of plastic whose power potential can be awesome. The only way to use credit cards intelligently is to pay off each month's balance, avoiding the outrageously high interest charges. But even paying on time doesn't always guarantee perfection.

You are dealing with computers when you use credit cards. God help you if the computer rings you up as owing more money than you do or if the computer slaps you with late payment, resultng in an interest charge. Yes, there are consumer-protection laws designed to help you. But as more than a few people will tell you, there is often a great deal of difference between principal and principle.

Kathy Ross had a bad time with a magazine-subscription service through which she ran a credit-card charge. Not only did her new subscriptions get mixed up with renewals, but she was charged for items she never ordered. She followed the consumer-protection rules, and within seven months she was being billed for fifty dollars in interest charges alone, still didn't have the subscription mess straightened out, and was getting dunning letters from the charge-card company, calling her irresponsible. Computers didn't understand her human pleas for logical service. Kathy never did get justice. She paid the charges, finally giving up because "it was easier."

If you can get the mark's credit-card number, order a huge bunch of mail-order merchandise for him/her. Use the telephone to order things too. The secret here, according to a former security agent for one of the card companies, is to keep the amount of each individual purchase under forty dollars, because telephone confirmations are made on greater amounts. Just make hundreds of forty-dollar purchases in a short time.

Using the mark's credit-card information to place telephone orders involves some investigation, according to Robert Schuster, a master manipulator. Sometimes, Schuster will simply call the mark's home, pretending to be a verification clerk at some local credit union or bank. Schuster gives the mark's full name and address, then asks the mark or the mark's spouse to please verify the credit-card numbers. If it works, and Schuster says it does ninety-nine percent of the time, you are now ready to simply order and order and order all sorts of goods and services on behalf of the mark.

If you have his/her credit-card number and you feel honest, don't steal with it. Go a step beyond and report the mark's card as stolen. Pretend you are the mark. That will cause some upset for the real mark when he/she tries to use the card a week or so later.

This is fraud, but one recycled Yippie who is now billed as a professional psychic for the various supermarket tabloids told me how he applied for and got various credit cards by lying on his application. Easily getting cards, he would run the credit to the extreme and beyond on the cards, survive the corporate dunning letters, then move to a new location without benefit of forwarding address. Despite my doubts, several corporations I asked denied that they passed along these losses to the rest of us in the form of outrageous interest charges.

Delivery of Consumables

For years kids have ripped off beer distributors' trucks, pizza wagons, etc. The scam is to call the place from a pay phone and give them a fake name in some high-rise apartment. Give them the pay-phone number and stick around there for a while, since some places call back to confirm orders. When the truck arrives with the order, and while he is up there trying to find a nonexistent customer, you could help yourself to what's left in the truck.

Why would anyone rip off an innocent beer-delivery truck or pizza wagon? Fred Littman has one reason, saying, "I ordered a pizza at one place locally, and it was awful. I spoke with the manager, and he told me to get lost and refused to give me my money back. I figured I had some free pizza coming to make up for that."

Lefty Gaylor has another reason: "We swipe beer from only one distributor, because everyone knows he's a big Mafia type, and they rip off everyone else, so why not steal from them?"

Isn't stealing from the Mafia dangerous?

"Not if you don't get caught, and this one's too dumb to know any better. He blames the drivers, and they get mad and figure if they're gonna get blamed, they might as well steal beer from him. That way we multiply our efforts."

Perhaps the Justice Department could find some use for Lefty and his boys.

Dirty Old Men

If you know some jerk who's a terminal lecher, not just a dirty old man, but a truly, grossly obnoxious swine, the following is a sure-fire method that's right on target. You need either three or four associates, depending on whether you personally want to go into the field on this one. One of your associates must be comely young lady.

The drill goes like this. The mark is told about the young lady. She is described as being either an unfaithful wife or a hot-to-trot daughter, depending on the age and circumstance. The mark is told she has eyes and everything else for him, and that if he wants to have a lot of heavy action, you or an associate will make the introduction.

As you approach the fateful house on the evening decided upon, you or your associate, acting as "guide," must stress that the husband or father is a fiery and jealous man and that she takes you on as a secret lover because of insatiable lust, etc. Build up both the sexual suspense and the thrill of the forbidden. You have to get his adrenaline and imagination cooking really well.

The mark and his guide are at the door and the sweet young thing opens it and moans out a greeting. She should be dressed—or undressed—in an appropriate fashion. The mark should have just enough time to wet his lips and survey her architectural lines. About the time his eyes bug is time for the next act.

Instantly, a large man comes roaring around the corner of the house, bellowing in rage about the honor of his wife or daughter. The guide screams in shrill terror, "Run! Run like hell! It's the husband [or father]!"

As the mark and guide start to dash away, a couple of shots are fired, and the guide falls. As he falls, he screams to the mark, "Jesus, keep running! He's killed me!" Another shot rings out; then all is silent.

All is not really silent. The mark's heart is probably thudding against his chest like a caged elephant. It's a great idea to carry on with this scenario for a few days, with you or another conspirator, who has been undercover, keeping the mark apprised of the guide's condition from the supposed gunshot wound. It would also be good to float the rumor that the father or husband is spending all his time looking for "the other bastard who got away."

The mark won't stop his fearful shakes long enough to wonder why the police haven't arrested the husband or father. Maybe, when he does come to this logical question, he will call the police and ask for protection. This scam turns a lot of corners before the mark finally realizes that he's been had. The police probably won't be as amused as you are, but you'll not know about that. The mark will.

If you know the right street people, and if you're going into dirty tricks you must know them, you will have trickster access to ladies with social diseases. Some of the veterans of the streets will help you out between treatments for a price. Younger, less-experienced ladies don't know they have the diseases, but their pimp or madam does. Think how much fun it would be if you could hire one of these venereal versions of Typhoid Mary to dazzle, pick up, and seduce your mark. This scam has been pulled off successfully by at least four people I know personally. It is not that hard if you plan, bargain, and buy ahead.

Drugs

Once, a very close friend of mine was badly hurt by a former employee who not only had been stealing from the company, but when the employee left, she said and did some terrible things that damaged my friend personally and professionally. Revenge was the best medicine, and he did extract his dose.

He waited a year to get even. It was worth it. The woman had moved to another job in a city about two hundred miles away, in the next state. Having access to drugs, my friend got a small amount of cocaine and planted it in her car during a special visit to the other city for just that purpose. He then used a pay phone to call police and give them the lady's name. He told them that she'd burned him on a drug deal and that he was turning her in because of it.

As this is written, the case is going to court. Happily for my friend, this female actually had a bit of marijuana on her person when she was busted for the planted coke. Talk about good luck. The third stroke of luck was that this bust took place in New York State. He has followed the case through the other city's newspaper and through a friend. He says the police aren't buying her story of innocence. The best part is that by now, she can't think of anyone who would have a motive to hurt her.

Having drugs around is a very dangerous risk. But if the stakes are right, it can become very serious business for the mark. You should know that your call to the police will be recorded. Disguise your voice mechanically by using a rerecording tape, or inhale some helium from a balloon just before you make the call, since it will alter your voice totally. If you're a good thespian, try to use a foreign or regional accent. Speak very softly, also. Don't stay on the line more than thirty to forty-five seconds. Do your number and hang up.

An old head like William Harvey would get a chuckle from this, if he were still with us to enjoy it. If his mark was straight or naïve about dope, Bill thought it was fun to mail him/her bagfuls of chopped weeds, oregano, etc., with some incense sprinkled on for scent. As an added touch he included one or two joints rolled using the bogus weed, with a note saying, "Enjoy the samples on me."

These materials were mailed to the mark's home address using a slight variation in the spelling of the name. Ideally, the mark thought she/he had been confused as an innocent dupe in a dope deal. After a day or two, Harvey had a male with a rough, raspy voice call the mark to ask if some package had been misdirected to him/her by accident. The caller suggested that other, nastier accidents might happen if the mark did anything uncool like calling the authorities. Naturally, the mark had already done this. What would you expect a mark-type person to do? After all, that's how people get to be marks.

As a postgraduate version of this scam, Harvey used to send a package containing a couple of hypodermic needles and some suspicious-looking white crystalline powder (sometimes with a touch of brown) using the same bit just described.

Environmental Rapists

If you dislike land rapists, such as developers, big real estaters, gas and oil drillers, etc., your first order of business is to read Edward Abbey's *The Monkey Wrench Gang,* twice. The first time you read for fun and pleasure; the second reading might be for tactics, as in a manual. For example, if you've had unpleasant dealings with utility companies "creating progress" in your area, for example, building roads, drilling gas or oil wells, stripping coal, deep mining, etc., you know the feelings. The monkey wrenchers have an answer.

Note the advice of one of Abbey's protagonists: "Always pull up survey stakes. Anywhere you find them. Always. That's the first goddamned general order in this monkey wrench business. Always pull up survey stakes."

He should have added that you should always replace the dirt from the stake hole, tamp it down, and disguise the scar, so the enemy cannot simply replace the stake. A further suggestion would be to move the survey stakes ... perhaps enough that a lawsuit could be instituted against the environmental rapists.

According to a Cat operator I shared several lemonades with a few times, Karo syrup poured into the fuel tank of heavy machinery is enough to deadline the equipment for a thorough bit of maintenance.

"It'll turn to solid carbon, that syrup, and seize the engine up tight. It makes a helluva mess of an engine. I'd suggest about three or four quarts per tankful.

"Now look, though," he cautioned, his eyes glinting hard enough to stare open clam shells at a hundred yards, "if you did that to my own machine I'd come after you hard. But if it was a company machine or if they'd leased my machine, hell, I'd probably buy you a drink afterward!"

In the summer of 1978, about 150 angry farmers in Minnesota held a beer-and-hot-dog party to celebrate the coming of the "bolt weevils." The party and the "weevils" cost a utility giant a quarter of a million dollars.

The farmers were fighting mad over the invasion of the huge utility conglomerates who were running their power towers and lines across the countryside, ruining farms and dairy operations. All legal and moral efforts to oppose this land rape failed. That's when the "bolt weevils" came to the farmers' rescue.

After beating off state police by using Wrist Rocket slingshots to fire ball bearings at patrol-car windows, the farmers brought out their wrenches and cutting tools. Soon, two of the 150-foot-tall, hundred-thousand-dollar transmission towers lay smashed on the ground, victims of the "bolt weevils."

A dozen years ago, these farmers were staunch, conservative Americans, firmly behind "their" government and its war. They were love-it-or-leave-it folk. Today, they are fighting mad at the establishment's government, and they claim that the radicals of the sixties were right. That's comforting, at last.

One farmer says, "The goddamn government's playing red herring, bleating about Arab terrorists and weathermen and the underground. Hell, it's the people—us, the little people—they better watch out for. We're the revolutionaries, and we're ready to fight.

"They may finish this power line and others, but the greedy, land-raping bastards will never keep it in operation. There's not enough guards for that. And more people are coming around to our way."

You could almost hear an echo of "All power to the people," with no hint of a pun.

A major gas company was ripping and raping all over the countryside, using the national need for natural gas as its excuse for avarice. One landowner whose livestock were disrupted by the gas-drilling operation decided to get even, quietly.

Farmer Dale explained, "I knew a little bit about the state environmental regulations, so I decided to help the gas company violate as many of them as I could, even if it meant sacrificing a few things of my own.

"Late one evening, I kicked over the hose from their fuel tank and opened the valve. By morning, the result was nearly seven hundred gallons of diesel fuel in the stream below my place. It took members of the sportmen's club about a mile down stream two hours to get state officials out there to the well site. Because of a phone call I'd made earlier, the local newspaper sent a reporter, too.

"Later that day, I dumped my barrel of old crankcase oil on the drilling access road, and you should have seen the foreman's pickup when it hit that oil. He slammed through my cornfield. I acted really wild, raising hell about first polluting our stream, then wrecking my crops and spilling oil on the road. He was shook up to beat hell and blamed his own truckers for leaking oil. I billed their company for three-hundred dollars in damages, and he endorsed the bill for payment right there."

Farmer Dale did some other things that week, like move and replace those "Underground Cable" markers used by power and phone companies to mark buried wires. Naturally, the driller's dozer tore up the real wires, creating further havoc. He sprayed weed killer on his own crops within a hundred-yard radius of the gas well, then raised royal hell with the state agricultural people. He submitted a bill for a thousand dollars for damaging his crops, although the gas company balked—at first.

"Finally, I dumped some chemicals in my old well and had the water tested (he had had the water tested prior to the drilling, of course) by the county. They reported it had gotten polluted during the time the gas well was being drilled. I turned it all over to my attorney at this time."

His attorney filed to have the drilling permit revoked and also to sue the company for huge damage settlements. The case was settled out of court, allowing the company to finish its rape, yet at a very high price, including unlimited free gas and a lot of cash for Farmer Dale.

Another combatant in the never-ending war between land rapists and landowners or environmentalists borrowed the old OSS tire-spike idea, married it to the Malay gate of Indochinese fame, and put some heavy vehicles on the shelf for a while. Angered because the well drillers for a natural-gas company were filling their mammoth water-tank trucks from a trout stream that ran through his property, a landowner spiked their plans. He took a two-inch-thick piece of twelve-inch board and pounded five ten-inch housing spikes through it. The board was about eighteen inches long. He did the same thing to another board.

The ambush site was the deeply rutted pull-off spot the heavy water trucks used when they sucked thousands of gallons of good water from the clean stream. The giant trucks had callously dug deep ruts, which filled with water from their sloshing loads. Our combatant placed his spiked boards, tips upward, into the ruts. He did this on a random schedule over a one-month period, disabling a total of seven trucks and finally forcing the land rapists and their trucks to another fill-up point.

As a postscript, he enjoyed this activity so much that he built dozens of the spike devices and became a traveling one-man hit squad, placing the traps whenever he saw evidence of the heavy water-tank trucks.

Explosives

Now that the feds have outlawed fireworks, you'd better save all the M80s you can find. Extremely versatile devices, M80s are excellent propellants for other substances. For example, this stunt started out as a dorm prank at Clapper Packer University but soon escalated into more deadly sport, which went like this. Put some fresh feces, the looser the better, into a large Baggie. Gently break the glass on a large-wattage lightbulb, but do not disturb the filament. Even more gently attach the filament to the fuse of the M80. Screw the bulb carefully back into a ceiling socket. Finally, move the bag of feces up and around the light fixture. Be certain the fuse and filament do not touch the feces, but see that the M80 is into the substance. Tape the bag to the ceiling.

Naturally, all this presupposes you have access to the mark's room or to a room where the mark is likely to be the one who comes in and turns on the light. One cautionary note: Be sure the light switch is off when you screw in the bulb. If it's not, you have about four seconds to avoid getting nasty coverage from the M80's blast. Done correctly, this is a spectacular stunt. As the designer of this one, George Dierk adds, "You don't have to limit your spatter substance to feces. Paint, cheap perfume, acid, and CS gas all have their place."

Gunpowder has a lot of uses in addition to filling up a portion of cartridges. If your mark has an outdoor barbecue, you could sprinkle a cup of old-fashioned black powder around the bottom of the grill. When the powder ignites it will do so with a huge, whooshy flash, accompanied by a great white cloud of smelly smoke. I would hate to imagine the multiple effects of such a pyrotechnical display on one of those fancy grills powdered by LP gas. Wow!

Don't let your imagination rest with the cookout grill. Remember fireplaces, wood stoves, ovens, etc. The experts suggest you use black powder rather than the more modern smokeless powders. Black powder really works!

If you can't get a regular smoke-bomb device, a smoke grenade, or something real from the military, make your own. According to Doctor Abraham Hoffman, the noted chemist, you combine four parts sugar to six parts saltpeter (potassium nitrate). You heat this mixture over a very low flame until it starts to blend into a plastic substance. When it begins to gel, remove it from the heat and allow it to cool. He suggests you stick a few wooden match heads into the mass while it's still pliable. You also add a fuse at this point. The smoke device is nonexplosive and nonflammable. But a pound of this mixture will produce enough thick smoke to cover a city block. Watch which way the wind blows.

John E. Warrenburger likes to mess up people's nervous systems. One of his favorite nonlethal tricks involving nonexplosives is a good bit of cardiac theater.

John says, "I bundle a few of those road flares—the ones in the red jackets—together and wrap them with black plastic tape. Connect this with some coiled wiring to a ticking alarm clock and place it so your mark will get the full visual and aural effect."

Applause, applause, John. Only God and the mark's launderer will know how dastardly the frightening effect of the bogus bomb is on the mark's nervous system.

Fillers

Trickster Aynesworth Belin is thrilled with the recent introduction of the super-foam products. These are urethane-and-resin compounds, usually in a spray can, which billow out and expand into a mass at least thirty times the original volume. They harden quickly, often within five minutes. Another version is a two-part liquid that when mixed does even more astounding things. One quart will give you the equal of 150 pounds of plaster.

A gallon of super foam will make eight cubic feet of the ultrastrong material, which is water, erosion, and corrosion proof, as well as heat and cold resistant. The irony is that these products have been marketed by major corporations for various legitimate filler jobs. They rely on advertising and societal brainwashing to make certain the lulled citizens use the product only for its duly intended purpose. If there was ever a product that belongs in the arsenal of the dirty trickster, this one is it. I took an informal survey of fifteen hardware stores in my area. All had the product in stock. Yet one clerk told me, "Most [buyers] are young kids . . . got no good use to mind."

I bet some of them have a very good use to mind. What can I say but, "Try it, you'll like it," even if the mark won't?

Forgery

Forgery is a fine art form, very useful to the trickster. During World War II, for example, the British Security Coordination often forged letterheads, documents, and official cables to thwart Hitler's efforts in the early dark days of 1939 through 1941. Some of their efforts were spectacular, especially in South America, working covertly with sympathetic American officials, officially neutral at that time. Some of their tactics are highly adaptable to today's dirty trickster. Full details are yours for the reading in *A Man Called Intrepid.* Another excellent reference is *The New Paper Trip,* which will give you everything you need to know about forging to get even.

Garage Sales

Ever have a garage sale? Ever been to one? They're incredible, and they seem to bring out the most in the worst people. Even I, a thick-skinned, terminal misanthrope, was awed at the gall of some people who demand to see your entire house or who pound on your door at 6:00 A.M. to get a "head start" on a garage sale you announced in the paper as starting at 9:00 A.M. Getting the message?

Let's have a garage sale at your mark's residence. Or let's have it in your mark's name but at the neighbor's address. List all sorts of outlandish bargains and tell people you have guns, old china, glassware, and dozens of inexpensive antiques. You want obnoxious gawkers, not buyers. Remember that! Naturally, the mark and/or the neighbor will know nothing of this until the first knock on the door at 6:00 A.M.

"I used to get all sorts of odd-hour calls from home-remodeling and -repair salespeople at this one local company," recalls Jim Kenslogger. "I must have called them a half dozen times to ask that my name and number be removed from their files. No luck. So I decided to change my luck.

"I learned who their chief executive was and pulled the bogus-garage-sale number on him, complete with newspaper ad. Then I started calling his home at odd hours, asking if he were the party having the garage sale. He was really out of sorts after about a week of this.

"I stopped, and about ten days later I got another routine sales call from his company. I called right back, asked to speak to that executive, and told him I was damn tired of being bothered by his salespeople and could he get them to stop calling me. He pledged he would and told me wearily, 'Buddy, I know just how you feel. I'll surely take care of it for you.' I had no trouble after that, so neither did he."

Gases

A serious dirty trickster should have a supply of ammonium sulfide. This liquid is loads cheaper to buy than milk, booze, or gasoline. It smells so awful that no one, not even the most terminal of coke sniffers, can stand to be around it once it has been brought into play. It may be sprayed or vaporized. Using this stuff as a base, Kurt Saxon offers a very effective formula for making your own stinkum in his book *The Poor Man's James Bond*. The stuff is so potent that it should have to be registered somehow with someone. Phew. But it's easy to make, and as long as it's harassing your mark's glands, what do you care?

A little leave-behind hostess present can be a small, uncapped bottle of butyric acid. Propped near the door you're closing, it will be knocked over when the mark enters the room. Phew.

Crowd-dispersal devices are also good choices for the trickster's arsenal. These include spray cannisters, gas grenades, pens, and other chemical-dispensing weapons. Many of these items may be purchased over the counter in some states. They're sold openly under a variety of trade names and generally contain CS gas, which is a military version of tear gas. If you can obtain it without undue risk, MACE is an excellent choice. Many manuals tell you how to make your own MACE.

You can buy many of these materials by mail order. Check current shipping regulations and any laws against these devices in your own area first, of course. One of the best mail-order companies in this business is American Colonial Armament, P.O. Box F, Chicago Ridge, Illinois 60415. If you are or can appear to be a law-enforcement official you can have access to a veritable smorgasbord of sophisticated gas weapons by getting a catalog from the F. Morton Pitt Company, at 1444 S. San Gabriel Blvd., San Gabriel, California 91776. Finally, if you prefer to brew up your own gases, get a copy of Kurt Saxon's classic book *The Poor Man's James Bond.* He tells you how to do it all in your own kitchen workshop. You can get his book from Atlan Formularies, P.O. Box 438, Eureka, California 95501.

From Elmer Bill, our gardening editor, comes the charming advice that spray cans of Raid and other insecticides provide you with an improvised defensive weapon. The stuff burns the eyes badly and will fire an eight- to ten-foot spray.

This buffet of gaseous ideas is method only. The rationale behind why you would use such tactics is your own business, of course. But at times when people or institutions have done you dirty—a dose or so of noxious gas may help set the record straight for you.

Graffiti

Contrary to popular belief, some people—usually the creepy ones you want for this stunt—do call names and numbers found in bar restrooms. Harvey Rankin and Festerwald Ray proved this premise in their study *Scrawl on the Wall*. What you learn from them is that you should write your mark's spouse's first name and phone number and a boldly stated sexual attraction (use your imagination) in every restroom of every bar in town. Biker and Jock bars are usually the best.

As a follow-up, you can tune in your tape deck to a pop country song, call the number yourself, and sound drunk. If you're lucky, the mark will answer. Tell the mark why you're calling and where you got the name and number. It is hoped that you'll be the only ringer among a large crowd of real callers.

Commercial graffiti are available in a form known as billboards and posters. You could have posters or billboards printed to announce your mark's coming out of the homosexual closet. Or your bogus billboard could announce a conservative political candidate's personal advocacy of gun control, gay rights, blacks, Chicanos, abortion, etc. Your political candidate may actually support busing. If so, your billboard for him should indicate his violent opposition to it. And so on.

Bumper stickers are another form of graffiti. You can get bogus ones printed in the same manner as billboards and posters. Or you can use legitimate bumper stickers for illegitimate purposes, such as slapping strongly adhesive bumper stickers that champion your political candidate—mark to the painted rear-deck surfaces of automobiles in a shopping-mall lot. It might be fun sometime to sit around thinking up other creatively rotten things you could do with bumper stickers to get even with someone.

For example, you could get bumper stickers printed that say, GAY IS GREAT . . . TRY IT, and place these on the automobiles of local bikers, right wingers, clergy, and others who feel threatened by homosexuals. You could get bumper stickers that say, HONK IF YOU'RE AN ASSHOLE TOO, and put them on the autos of marks whom you feel are qualified. BAN HANDGUNS or HUNT HUNTERS bumper stickers go great on the property of redneck gun nuts. Or put NRA FOREVER! and JUST TRY TO TAKE MY GUN AWAY! on the property of the simple and misguided wimps who really think gun control serves any useful purpose.

Other fun bumper stickers can say things like, BEER DRINKERS GET MORE HEAD; SUCK MY TAILPIPE; HONK IF YOU'RE HORNY; HOORAY FOR THE KKK; or DEUTSCHLAND ÜBER ALLES. Stickers featuring swastikas or Soviet flags can also be used creatively.

Highways

An activist can have fun on the roadway, too. Can you imagine the damage possible if one were to substitute a road sign that read, GROSS WEIGHT 15 TONS, for the original sign on a bridge approach that read, GROSS LOAD 5 TONS? One protesting employee did this at his employer's Ohio plant and had materials shipments shut down for eight days.

In World War II, it was common for enemy agents on all sides to turn road signs so as to misdirect military convoys, screwing up operations. The same tactic could be used today, even if your only enemy is some governmental branch or agency.

In the annals of highway history no one has seen the equal of the many low points of the Pennsylvania Department of Transportation, traditionally a repository for political hacks, Mafia underlings, patronage hogtroughers, and the terminally incompetent. M. Harvey Shopp, a veteran political trickster, has all sorts of suggestions for highway fun such as painting sawhorses to look like official blockades and using them to close highways, bridges, etc.

Another of Shopp's ideas is to produce bogus DETOUR signs and place them at strategic locations where they will be sure to screw up highway traffic.

The road woes of Allen McDonald illustrate the

rationale behind these moves. Whenever the county in which he lived did road repair to a bridge near his home, they always parked their equipment in his yard. When county road scrapers went by, they piled a line of debris high enough to close his driveway. In winter, they also closed his own freshly shoveled driveway, this time with ice-hard snow and frozen slush. All calls to county officials were answered only with uncaring and operationally impotent cluckings of the tongue.

"I decided to return some of the favors," McDonald said. "I began to turn road and other directional signs around. I stole a couple of BRIDGE OUT signs in another county and placed them in front of perfectly good bridges in our county. I once called the local radio station and announced several road repairs that would mandate detours—telling them I was a county road super, of course—which really screwed up local traffic for a couple of days.

"The upshot is that the county got a lot of nasty calls and even more bad media publicity, and the county commissioners agreed to investigate these problems 'caused' by the road people. Naturally, in the midst of all this I also brought up my beefs about their conduct, offering to testify at the hearings. All abuses against my property quickly stopped. So I stopped my counter-abuse program."

Check the "Joggers" section of this book to learn about the use of the OSS tire spikes of World War II infamy.

Hookers

In many cities independent business people have set up a personal service whose employees make housecalls. These paid friends come in all sexes and meet all tastes. It might be fun to invite one of these hedonistic harlots to "your" house. Use the mark's name and a neighbor's address. Try to pick the most upright, puritan neighbor you can find to receive this sexual good Samaritan—a professional virgin or librarian; something on that order.

Not all prostitutes carry the Good Housekeeping Seal; some carry venereal diseases. These are fairly common among streetwalkers, the bargain basement of hookerdom. If you or a trusted friend in law enforcement, medicine, or social service can locate one of these carnal carriers and your mark has a weakness for ladies, hire her and let her pick up your mark. Nature, as they say, will take care of the rest.

I'm certain your vengeful imagination will have no trouble matching a deserving mark with a paid friend who might give him/her more than bargained for. I know a couple of people who set up a cop this way. The cop was especially hypocritical and nasty about honest working girls: He'd fully and freely sample the services before busting and totally persecuting the servicer. He got his, so to speak.

Hotels

Suppose you are staying at a hotel and get into a bad beef over the poor quality of the meal you get in their restaurant. After trying to be reasonable, here is how Ralph Charell, a champion-class advocate for the little guy, handled it. Seeing absolutely no satisfaction and no end of snobbish treatment, Charell took the following steps. He requested a deposit box in the hotel safe and placed the offending rib roast, which he felt was of poor quality, in the box and locked it. The box had two separate locks and two separate keys. One was held by the hotel, the other by Charell.

"At this point, the hotel management had absolutely no idea what I'd placed in the box," Ralph Charell explained. "I told them it was valuable evidence in a possible legal action I was considering against an organization with whom I was having a disagreement about the quality of one of their products."

In a short time, someone at the desk caught the disagreeable odor of decay coming from the area of the safe. Within another short time, Charell was called by the manager and asked to clear whatever was in the box out of the box. Charell explained about the "evidence" in this legal action. The hotel manager threatened to force open the box anyway. Charell reminded him of the laws against destroying evidence, then explained the whole situation.

"What do you want from me, Mr. Charell?" was the manager's beaten reply.

Ralph Charell then reported the details of the dinner he and his party had had at the hotel. It takes a real expert like Ralph Charell to turn a trick into something positive for all sides.

In Homer City, Pennsylvania, a group of the locals told about the time a fellow had a room at a nearby boardinghouse. He was the pompous sort of smartass who just begged to be dirty tricked. The locals went to a junkyard and bought a huge gang plow. It was in pieces and was relatively easy for these husky lads to put in the mark's rooms. They assembled it and welded the pieces together with a small, portable machine. They and their machine left. There was a great deal of consternation on the part of the mark and the landlord, who parted company faster than the room and the plow. Automobiles and other bits of large machinery work equally well in rooms and apartments today.

A collegiate trick reported by Whitney Clapper called for hiding small dead things, such as mice, sparrows, or moles, in out-of-the-way places of the mark's rented room. Good secret places include light fixtures, inside switch boxes, unused overcoat pockets, and inside appliances. Within a few days the mark will be aware that something is wrong. A few more days, and he'll be sure. Left unattended, this stunt will provide the mark with a large mass of pet maggots to raise.

Homes

All sorts of things have homes—snails, snakes, groundhogs, weasels, Japanese beetles, even marks. One vengeful way of getting even with a mark is to destroy the moat to the castle of his/her home. The idea is to hit close to home, for both the physical and the psychological destruction involved.

One example started at the apartment of Pat Konely. Because the landlord refused to make needed roof repairs, several rainstorms flooded Konely's apartment, damaging personal property. The landlord also refused to pay damages, and Konely didn't have the money to fight the landlord's attorney.

Pat Konely admits the response wasn't very funny, but it did put a damper on the mark's day and his own home. It worked because the mark's front door had one of those mail slots cut in it. Konely says that this stunt works wonders when the mark is not aware of what's going on until the poor drip really gets the message. Here's what Konely suggests. Hook a hose, ideally the mark's, to the outdoor faucet. Unscrew the power nozzle so you have bare hose. Carry it to the mail slot and quietly fit the bare hose end through the slot and into the house. Got the picture? Good. Konely says you just turn on the faucet and hope the mark has slow reactions. Most tricksters would agree that it's hardly sporting to do this when the mark is away from home.

"That would be like shooting puppies in a barrel," Konely snorts. "At least tip the barrel over and give them a running start, so to speak."

If your mark hates cats, be sure to place dead fish in obscure and unpleasant places around his/her abode. Do this at night. If you want feline audio accompaniment, tie a large dead fish from a tree limb or pole just out of the reach of the neighborhood cats. The nearer to the mark's bedroom window, the better.

The modern epoxy glues are a miracle to many and a menace to others. The latter is exemplified by the exasperation of a person who's just discovered that someone has squirted a load of strong glue into her/his door lock. (Liquid solder works too.)

You know all those vents in the back and top of a television set? If you ever pour a bunch of iron filings down in there, some interesting things will happen to the mark's set the next time it is turned on.

How about some party humor? If your mark doesn't know you're getting back at him yet, you might even find yourself a guest in the target home. You could start off your festivities by quieting yourself away from the crowd, locating the family freezer, and either turning the unit down greatly, pulling the plug (unless it's equipped with a safety signal), or switching it to defrost.

A trickster by the name of Micki related how she once came bearing gifts for the mark's family freezer. She had matched the hostess's freezer wrapping paper and style perfectly. Then, nestled among the nice beef roasts, steaks, hamburgers, and chickens belonging to the mark, Micki added her own packages of frozen roadkill—dead cats, small dogs, groundhogs, and crows.

Happy eating, all you mystery-meat fans.

While doing your tour of the targeted facilities don't forget to dump some fiberglass or insulation dust into the mark's washing machine. It will be picked up by the clothes, ideally undergarments. Within half an hour of getting dressed, a person wearing clothing impregnated by the fiberglass or insulation dust will wish he/she weren't. It creates terrible itching that takes two or three days to disappear. The best part is that no one ever thinks to blame the rash on sabotaged clothing. Repeated doses of this stunt are enough to make a stong mark crumble. A continual supply of "product" is assured if you mix the nasty dust in with the laundry detergent.

Every real kid knows what sulfur smells like when burned—horribly rotten eggs. Once, some of my peer-group delinquents put three pounds of it in a nasty neighbor's furnace, after somehow gaining entry to the basement. The house had to be aired for nearly forty-eight hours. It was awesome. If you want some fireworks with your sulfur-in-the furnace gimmick, throw in a mixture of potassium permanganate and sugar. It will flare, smoke grandly, and, with the sulfur present, stink all the more.

Here is one of Leon Spectre's recipes for ill humor. He hopes you dig it.

Your mark (and family if there is one) is away for at least the weekend, and you know about it enough ahead that you can hire a backhoe operator. Also, rent a pickup truck and tape a cardboard sign to its door with some vague identification on it about a landscaping business. Smear the license plate with mud or borrow another plate for a short while.

You should arrive at the mark's house about half an hour before the backhoe. Naturally, you used the mark's name when you engaged the backhoe and you told the operator you'd have a landscape contractor (you) there to meet him. The neighbors should think everything is in order if you act as if you know what you're doing.

Don't give the backhoe operator a good look at you, and use some disguise kit if possible. The premise is that the mark wants to add a basement room somewhere on the house. You must tell the backhoe operator exactly where to excavate. In most suburban areas, underground utility lines are indicated with aboveground markers. You can pick up gas lines and water lines from the meters. Pick an area clear of utility lines and pipes and lay out some string and stakes. Do all this before your operator arrives. Tell him your client, the mark, wants that area excavated and to bill the mark directly. Further, tell him that you have to leave to pick up your foreman and crew and that you'll be back in about twenty minutes. Ideally, you'll never see the backhoe operator again.

As Frank Foge points out, "My chemistry teacher always said there'd be a practical use for these high school science courses someday." She was right. Do you remember what termites look like? Good. If not, any insect book will tell you. Or visit your local Orkin man and tell him you need to obtain some termite eggs for an experiment. Or get them from a science-supply house.

I bet you already know the experiment. It's called how fast can the little eggs hatch into hungry termites and devour the mark's house? There's no trick here; you just infest your mark's home with the little buggers. They'll do the rest. This last one was prompted by a frustrated renter whose landlady refused to have the cockroaches and other pests exterminated from an apartment. A serious illness to an infant child, traced directly to the landlady's refusal to follow sanitary laws, triggered the nasy "bugging" by the renter.

Insurance
Companies

In the intelligence business, access to insurance-company files is regarded as an operational goldmine. A former operative explains, "These files contained detailed analysis of actual and potential weaknesses, trouble spots, and other problems of any sort facing clients. Insurance companies stand to lose millions of dollars in the event of an actionable accident or difficulty, such as the Three Mile Island fiasco. Obviously, these very thorough and detailed investigative data would be of immense interest to a saboteur. In other words, these companies want to know the details by which anything and everything could go wrong with a client. These data are like a primer on sabotage."

Getting access to these reports and data may not be so easy for the nonprofessional. But if you have enough dedication and imagination you will find a method. The kids who blackbagged the FBI offices in Media, Pennsylvania, were nonprofessionals, and look what they pulled off! They managed to liberate entire files of illegal domestic espionage, which later blew apart COINTELPRO, the blackest eye Hoover's FBI ever suffered.

Now, let's get to the insurance companies themselves. Suppose you get turned down for insurance and you want to know why. By law, the insurance company must show you the file it has on you. Suppose you learn that all sorts of misinformation and other lies are in there. There are organizations and lawyers that deal in just that sort of thing, and a load of simultaneous lawsuits for such things as invasion of privacy and slander would be great.

Deborah Bodenhead hates junk mail, especially mail-order insurance hustles. So she answers these requests with affirmative orders; "I'll buy," she tells them. Then she runs salespeople and clerks through all sorts of scheduled, broken, rescheduled, rebroken, etc., appointments. She settles, finally, on a policy, then waits for the second billing to cancel. Why the second billing?

"They rarely send out the policy before the first billing," Deborah explains. "I want them to go to the expense of preparing and processing the policy. I usually get a second bill with a polite dunning letter. That's when I cancel. It drives the salespeople to anguish every time. Usually when they whine and ask me why, I tell them I really hate mail-order advertising and just decided to cancel on a matter of principle about junk mail."

I asked an insurance agent about this stunt, and he cursed people like Deborah, saying these people drove our rates up. I asked him if it wasn't really the companies' own obnoxious marketing techniques that drove up rates! He cursed me, too.

Don't ever feel pity or sorrow for insurance companies. They make more profit in an hour than any of us make in salary in a year.

IRS

A veteran dirty trickster named Michael Mertz has something good to say about the Internal Revenue Service—it can be used to furnish a hard time for your mark. Mertz knows his way around government agencies, and here's one of his IRS offerings.

"You'll need your mark's Social Security number and some other obvious personal data. Once you get those data you're on your way.

"Call a regional IRS office and 'confess' that you have cheated on your income tax, your conscience has bothered you, and you want to make things right by this great nation. Make an appointment with an auditor, using your mark's name, Social Security number, address, etc."

The kicker comes when the mark doesn't show up to keep the appointment, for obvious reasons. The IRS will send a visitor around to talk with the mark, and chances are he will be audited, regardless of his explanations.

So much for using IRS to hassle your mark. Many more folks would prefer the IRS were the mark. As in dealing with any large bureaucracy and its people, many of the stunts mentioned in other chapters may be brought to play against the IRS. However, there are a few specific tricks that might be used to bring rain on the IRS picnic.

You could start by picking up a bunch of blank returns and filing them in the names of your least favorite people.

I have been assured by a former IRS field auditor that someone will have to make an effort to verify each return.

With the help of your printer and your newly found forgery skills, prepare some financial documents indicating that some person or corporation has received some substantial income. Make copies of copies several times until you have a fifth- or sixth-generation copy that is not too clean but is still easily sharp enough to read. The idea is to make it look like copies of a purloined original. Call an IRS office from a phone booth and tell them you are an honest employee of the mark and you think he is evading taxes. Offer to send the IRS person the papers. Get off the phone very quickly, then send the papers. If the IRS gets nasty they may find themselves in court. I got this idea from a man who worked for a company that did fight IRS in court and won big—through an honest IRS error. Think what could happen to IRS if you fed them a dishonest error!

Thomas Jefferson

A quote by Thomas Jefferson can be used to confuse your friends or critics if they question your activities as a dirty trickster. A very sharp man who would be as upset with things in America as you are, Jefferson is quoted as saying, "Resistance to tyrants is obedience to God."

Let the authoritarians and their domestic gestapo choke on that one. It's enough to make them thump a few Bibles. What would be Thomas Jefferson's views on revolution, anarchy, busing, the draft, marijuana, and excessive taxation?

Joggers

Overweight and overwrought motorists drive by in their Detroit Dinosaurs, pass a jogger, and mutter, "Damn stupid schmuck." It's the human way to hate what and whom you don't understand. Joggers are often thought of as nuts, oddballs, and kooks to be dealt with.

Marty Jones, a landowner, is more specific, saying, "They run across a corner of my property, using a path I put in for my own use. I posted the land, but they ignored the postings. I have tried to talk to them, but they may or may not even stop to listen. If they stop they keep running in place while I'm raising hell about trespass. I think most joggers are rude, self-centered, and selfish. I was thinking about hiding in the bushes and ambushing them with my kid's BB gun."

For a variety of reasons, many people don't like joggers. Some folks even actively plot against joggers, using cars and motorcycles, then arming themselves with boards, pies, and other objects with which to strike the runners. There are less barbaric ways, however.

Tire spikes are a World War II relic. During the hostilities, they were dumped from low-flying aircraft onto enemy airfields and main transportation roadways, where they caused havoc. Your use might not be so widespread, but with equally exasperating results. The tire spike is a simply made piece of one-eighth-inch-thick steel cut in the form of a four-pointed star. Its purpose is to puncture rubber tires. The original wartime models were three inches in diameter and had four points at forty-five-degree angles. One of the points always stuck upward, ready to impale a vehicle tire. Even today, there are many uses for tire spikes.

One anti-jogger has already suggested that these spikes be reduced in size and dropped strategically near the running habitat of these long-range exercise buffs. The purpose, I presume, is to penetrate the expensive bottom of expensive jogging footwear and, perhaps, th expensive foot of the jogger. One critic called this tactic "a really sick pain in the metatarsus."

Ultrathin piano wire strung shin high on a pathway is excruciatingly nasty. That's another World War II stunt redrafted for this book by Colonel Jake Mothra. Many military manuals offer equipment and directions, he adds.

Another contribution to joggermania would be to sprinkle marbles on their special little pathways. Another nasty trickster, Hidell Crafard, told me about an acquaintance at the Hunt Sporting Club in Dallas who actually put ground glass into the running shoe of a bitter enemy. Perhaps that's where filet of sole originated.

There aren't many counteractivities a jogger can use in retaliation. One is to carry MACE for obvious use. Another tactic is to carry cans of garish-hued spray paint. These can be directed against attackers' automobiles.

Laundromats

In addition to using the dryer for a pizza oven, as outlined in another section of this book, you can either use laundromats to harass an individual mark, or the business itself can be your mark. It is not very hard, for example, to dump several packets of dye into someone's wash, ruining his/her clothing. Doing this at random will bring grief to the owners of the laundromat. One antisocial chap used to put small piles of moistened rust particles in the dryer used by his mark so the mark's clothing would have large rust stains. Roadkill may also be used to good advantage in these operations.

Additives that are positive ingredients for a good time at the laundromat include raw eggs, fish, peanut butter, and fiberglass. If your mark is the operator of the business, you will find a variety of his/her ancillary services to bugger, including vending machines, customer seats, and restrooms. Small nails or staples driven partly into chairs make good items for customers to snag themselves and their clothing on, for example. And vending machines can be made to steal money from patrons.

Lawn

Our outdoor correspondent, Lother Gout, came up with a scheme to hassle your mark's lawn. It's a simple matter of spilling quantities of tomcat lure on the targeted lawn. The urine of Felix Domesticus will do wonders for the lawn and the mark's disposition.

There are also a number of commercial lawn-care products that may be used to good advantage by the serious dirty trickster. One stunt is to select a large, open chunk of your mark's lawn. Using concentrated weed killer, you spell socially offensive words on the lawn with the defoliant. The grass dies, and a nasty word or legend is spelled out for all the neighbors to see. This works best on a slight slope facing a street for maximum exposure. Salt or vinegar will work almost as well as commercial vegetation killer. If you're the sort of fun person who's read this far, I'm certain you'll need no suggestions as to what to say in your little message.

Serious defoliation is one of the many techniques our Vietnam experiences made available to the dirty trickster. Defoliation is the most potent way to get back at dastardly people who also have unreasonable pride in their lawns and ornamentals. These are usually the type of fussy people who also own small, yipping, bitchy dogs the size of rats—more on that later.

This time we're going to take out everything that grows. There are many commercial products available that will kill anything growing. Look on the label to see that it says the stuff is nonselective and/or that it makes the soil barren. You just load up your sprayer—or the mark's, if you can get to it—and fire away. Like a good guerrilla, pick out what he loves most and hit it first and heaviest. Don't leave a single blade or stem standing. No prisoners. Be cautious, though, that you stay upwind from the spray. At night you can't tell how much of the gunk you are inhaling or getting on your skin. We have enough Agent Orange victims now without adding you to the list.

Reinhard Ray, a former special-operations man for the U.S. navy, suggests a selective use of the weed killer in a psychological battle against a mark who is a true worrier, fringing on paranoia. You apply the solution fairly heavily around the mark's natural or LP gas meter; then, broadcasting a bit more lightly, you follow the fuel line directly to the mark's house. A final, heavier dose would be appropriate at the jointure of home and line. Within a few days the frightened mark will be convinced that his entire gas system is leaking badly. Obviously, this is effective only if your mark uses natural or LP gas. But you could also do this to a water-supply line coming into the house or a buried electric line.

A related scam would be to spray the stuff in a circle around the house. Then, on bogus official letterhead you've either duplicated or had printed, send the mark a letter from the Nuclear Regulatory Commission explaining how they've just discovered some long lost records revealing that the mark's home was built over a former repository for nuclear wastes. I'm sure your imagination can embellish the rest of the letter's content to convince the mark that he, his family, and home are now radiation victims. Obviously, you can't use this if the mark's house is more than twenty years old, because nuclear waste dumps weren't built much before then.

Lawyers

Punxy Phil Ferrick decided to get back at a dishonorable attorney who decided to try hoodwinking the public by becoming a politician. Ferrick got hold of the attorney's legal letterhead and got it duplicated by a printer who was equally outraged at this crook's trying to capitalize his larceny by becoming an elected thing.

Using the letterhead for starters, Ferrick sent out blatant dunning letters over the mark's signature demanding campaign contributions from politically sensitive people. Another mailing was a group of threatening letters to local civic, church, and charity groups about their winked-at illegal bingo and 50/50 fundraisers. In the bogus letter, the lawyer threatened action.

The bogus mailings made the local newspaper when the lawyer—who had been a big booster, campaigner, organizer, etc., for Nixon in '68 and '72—complained of the dirty tricks. The newspaper treated the story straight: The attorney's denials only aroused more suspicion. And no one ever suspected Ferrick . . . until now.

Another scheme is this: Get a blank deed of trust, fill in your mark's name and address, use your notary seal, and you have a legitimate-looking phony document. File it at the courthouse, and you have an action in the works against your mark. It means the mark has defaulted on a mortgage or some other promissory note and that "you" are filing against it. "You" can be an attorney if you wish when "you" sign this form. Days of frustration, anger, and bureaucratic disbelief directed at the mark will follow before things are straightened out. Don't get caught doing this one. It is a serious no-no worth several penal slaps on the wrist. The best point here is that no one ever does things like this illegally, so the bureaucrats will never suspect it as a dirty trick.

But there's more. If you have access to a law library or law-library materials, you can play games with the mark's mind, claims Oswald Helms, an observer of the legal scene. He suggests, "Law libraries have standardized legal-practice forms, form books, and routine stationery forms that lawyers, clerks, judges, and the like use to help draft legal letters and proper legal forms. A dummy form or letter, photostated with some dummy legal notices, using, for example, arrest warrants, summonses, condemnations, search warrants, etc., can often pass for the real thing. It will shake the mark very much.

"The secret behind this," Helms explains, "is that real legal people sometimes use the Xerox machine and routine forms, too. It saves time and money. It will easily fool the target and will probably force his or her attorney to at least follow it up."

Time and money, time and money. Good torting.

License Plates

There are many sophisticated and clever ways to obtain additional vehicular license plates that aren't registered in your real name. However, it's not necessary to fool around with all that esoterica. Be like a street punk and simply steal what you need. A bad guy who needs a plate simply removes one from someone's car or truck. That simple. This is also highly illegal. But if you're careful and use a bit of common sense, can you think of a simpler and safer way of getting the extra plates you need for dirty tricks?

Ma Bell

Did you ever see those office signs that say, THINK? In one telephone-company office I visited, I saw signs saying, SNEER.

People have been messing with Ma Bell for as long as that corporate dictator has been monopolizing telephone service. For years stories have circulated about using strips of Scotch tape on coins, which allows their use again and again in pay telephones. Do you know what a number-fourteen washer will accomplish in a pay telephone?

The Yippies and other groups have developed marvelously ingenious ways of sabotaging telephone-company operations. Some of their literature is sheer technological genius, almost as if it were written by a Bell Laboratories dropout. I once spoke with a radical who had become a "mole," an agent of his political beliefs who secreted himself away in five years of deep cover working as a technician for Illinois Bell. His purpose was to learn about the technical side of the company so he could later control or destroy telephonic communication.

Gordon Alexander presents an alternative manner, simple but novel in these complex days. A professional dirty trickster for more than twenty years, Alexander uses the dangerous but simple method of physically cutting telephone lines. If you are looking for instructions on how to safely cut Ma Bell's lines here, forget it. Unless you know what you are doing and have the proper equipment you could easily light up like an insect hitting an electric bug trap. I said it was simple; I didn't say it was easy or safe.

Lee Jenner, an accountant, suggests that you overpay your telephone bill if you're alienated from Ma Bell. He says, "Overpay by a constant seventeen cents a month. Make it consistent. Then, after a few months, underpay by seventeen cents. Start another pattern for a while of overpayment; then underpay again. It drives them nuts."

Jenner continues, "The local telephone company had screwed a client of mine and refused to even give him the time of day. He started this seventeen-cent bit, and before the year was out he had the manager of the local company begging him to stop. It worked totally to his satisfaction."

Meanwhile, on other battlefield fronts, Bell-hater Leo Garry says you should have your printer make a bunch of OUT OF ORDER signs with the local Ma Bell's logo on them. Hang them on every public telephone you find. Speaking of pay telephones, only punks and idiots damage them. Much as you may hate them, they're the only game in town. If you've ever needed a pay phone in an emergency, you know what I mean.

You can play games with your local service representative (Ma Belltalk for salesperson) by ordering phones and equipment for marks or ordering service shutoffs. Always make these types of calls from a pay phone, for obvious reasons.

Bandit calling may have been developed by the Yippees. Certainly they are among its champions, both as practitioners and as cheerleaders. Aside from the blue boxes, which make free calls for you, there is a tactic that can be used by the nontechnical wizard and doesn't cost you anything. It's the use of the bogus credit-card numbers, and it works like this.

Always use a pay telephone and not always the same one. Next, you need a credit-card number. Here is where knowledge of Ma Bell's codes comes in. For that information check *Overthrow*, a tabloid published by the Youth International Party. A subscription costs you ten dollars a year, but each issue contains all sorts of other dirty tricks, as well as an updated listing of not only Ma Bell's codes, but also the complete credit-card numbers for many corporations, public utilities, and government agencies. To order a subscription, send ten dollars to Overthrow, P.O. Box 392, Canal Street Station, New York, N.Y. 10013. It's a good investment, according to most readers.

After you get credit-card codes or numbers, the Yippees claim, the rest of bandit calling is simple. You simply dial the long distance operator from your pay phone and sound very, very businesslike when you say, "This is a credit card call, and my number is [give the operator the credit-card number]. I want to call [give the operator only the number of the party you are calling]." Be sure you can tell a suspicious operator the area code from which the card was supposedly issued. If the operator wants to know who holds the card, either make up a legitimate-sounding company name or use the name of the agency or company whose card number it really is, depending upon the circumstance. It helps if your party at the other end of the call knows what's happening.

Talk straight and businesslike for the first five minutes, as a snoopy operator—that's the way Ma Bell trains them—might stay on the line that long to listen in. Avoid sensitive subjects like your name, politics, drugs, or dirty tricks, since you never know who is recording calls these days. Break off the call within twelve minutes. Obviously, your callee should act very dumb when Ma Bell's security people do come to investigate a month or so after the fraud is discovered. And don't let them intimidate you or your friends, either. They're good at that—many of them are former federal or state police.

One Bell employee told me that their security people utilize warrantless wiretaps, blackmail, and physical surveillance to catch persons suspected of making bandit calls. The employee also told me these tactics are used against persons who even *publicize* such practices. I consider myself warned. So should you. Ma Bell can be one nasty mother.

By the time you read this, though, the game may be up. In Washington state, the Supreme Court there upheld the conviction of a newspaper for publishing the telephone company's secret codes. The telephone company, which has both security and propaganda sections that rival the government's, was working furiously behind the scenes to influence the verdict.

Abbie Hoffman suggested this next trick, so if it doesn't work, call him. Restrict Hoffman's idea to corporate, utility, or institutional telephone systems. Cut the female end off an ordinary extension cord. Unscrew the mouthpiece on the telephone in any one office. You will see a terminal for a red wire and one for a black wire. Attach one of the wires from the extension cord to the red and one to the black. Finally, plug the extension cord into a power socket.

According to Hoffman, you are sending 120 volts of electricity back through equipment designed for six volts. He says this will knock out thousands of other telephones and the main switchboard, "if all goes right." Even if his numbers are somewhat exaggerated, you've had a good day.

Mail

The Ku Klux Klan has some interesting strategies for spreading terror. One of these is to collect from regional newspapers clippings of unsolved arsons (or robberies, rapes, burglaries, assaults, etc.). If you need to fatten the file, include clips from national publications too. Place the clips in a manila envelope and tape it to an old gasoline can (or ax, bra, shotgun shell, jimmy bar, etc.), which you leave on your mark's home or office doorstep.

David Williams is the pen name of a Texas state legislator who spends his working hours as a freelance writer. He told about Jim Boren (pen name of a friend), whose great idea for practical joking was to send single-entendre postal cards bearing personal, sexual, or medical messages to Williams's home.

"Since I met Jim Boren, I hide from my postman," Williams notes.

Williams is not Boren's only victim. Many of his friends suffer from postal cards such as the bogus Playboy Towers Memo that pointed out, "Davie Boy, thanks for taking care of my friend while she was in Austin. I was envious when she told me how things went down. Love, Elvira."

Or this hotel postcard from Hong Kong, addressed to Williams via his pen name at his real address: "She's no longer at the topless bar. But her sister at the massage parlor thinks she went to Seoul. I can pursue it at the embassy, but will have to disclose your personal interest. Please advise."

It is signed by a J. Harley, identified by a return address as "Harley's Detective Agency" in New Orleans. There is no Harley, no agency, no nothing at the return address.

Jim also sends cards to people's wives. One said: "Sorry, just couldn't make it this time. My wife came along."

One of Harley's better efforts at postal assassination was this gem, sent from Toronto: "Thanks for your help with the bail money. You done better by me than President Nixon did by his boys for doing about the same thing. If I get the book thrown at me later, I'll ride it out, but I want a written agreement on the money and I don't want you saying ugly things about me in the papers if they learn about your personal role in this."

From Cleveland, Jim Boren sent David Williams this postcard: "The cops found your name and address in one of the girls' diaries. They may be in touch soon. —A friend."

This next stunt is also accomplished through the mail. Posing as a medical researcher, Elmer Surehe says, you can probably con some crablice eggs from a supply house, for a price, of course. The eggs are inserted with an innocuous business letter into an envelope addressed personally to the mark. When the mark opens and unfolds the letter, the lice eggs drop onto his/her clothing and surroundings.

It would make sense that nothing in this letter connect back to you, of course. Some people have used the name and return address of another mark. The resulting confusion will ensure that two marks are unhappy.

A critic felt that this tactic would be unfair because an innocent secretary, business associate, or spouse might intercept the letter and receive the dose. Two observations—first, people shouldn't read personal mail addressed to other people; and second, sometimes the innocent must scratch along with the guilty.

A pulled-punch version of the lice-eggs letter is to use

itching powder instead. It's easily available from novelty stores, or you can make your own following the directions printed in some of the formula books available. Sneezing powder is another alternative.

A suggestion for a nastier ingredient came in from a former agent of the American intelligence community who got paid a lot of money for planning and implementing things like this. He suggests a chemical tear-gas powder heavily laced into an envelope, noting, "It will clear a mailroom or an office in minutes."

Mail Drops

These are essential if you're going to carry on any sort of correspondence with a mark or with suppliers of services and equipment. Depending upon the circumstances, you will need either a postal box or a regular street-address mail drop. Post-office boxes may be obtained in any name, although you will have to present some identification documenting your "identity."

If your scam is a short-termer, pick an apartment with many little boxes. Choose an empty one, claim it for the duration, and have it checked daily. Put in your little name card and use that exact address on your returns. The mail-delivery person doesn't know or care who comes and goes. Or you can have a very cool and trusted friend front their address for you as a mail drop. However, this person must be prepared and capable of carrying off a very plausible denial. You'd better think this one through before involving another person. Deniability can be a tough rap for an amateur.

Marriage

Marriage (catch)

Carol Sludge and a friend decided they should stage manage an entire wedding for a mark. So they did. She handled the gown and the bridesmaids' goodies, and he did the sartorial bit for the men. They got invitations and arranged for a church, a reception hall, a caterer, and an orchestra. They did it all in the name of the mark and his fictitious spouse to be. They chose a time when the mark was on vacation to send out invitations for the Sunday the mark was due back in town. Everyone showed up for the ceremony—everyone but the "bride and groom." Guests were somewhat miffed, and merchants and others descended upon the mark at his place of business Monday morning, wanting to be paid for goods and services.

Beyond that, what do you turn to after the standard old buns of wrecking the marriage ceremony have been batted around the bachelor-party table? Here are some quickie suggestions, brought to you by the Reverend Robby Gayer:

1. Hire a woebegone lady with a young child to troop into the reception and confront the groom-mark with the question of his continued child-support payments.

2. Hire an outstandingly healthy young wench who is just brimming over with sensual physical charm. She should cause heads to turn if she's costumed correctly as she vamps up to the groom-mark and plants wet soul

kisses on him, cooing, "Don't forget our past, love. And when you're tired of that little girl next-door, you know where to find me." As she leaves, she stage whispers, "Last [night, week, whatever] was just super. Don't be a stranger—you're too much man for that."

3. Call the church office before the ceremony and say that a crazed ex-lover of the bride plans to destroy the reception. Just as the reception begins, arrange to have many M80s or grenade simulators exploded.

4. Consider bringing additives into play with the punch and the food.

5. Hire someone, grief stricken at the loss of the bride or groom, to messily and dramatically "attempt suicide" at either the ceremony or the reception. Be sure to have associates to carry the victim out quickly for "medical attention."

6. Hire someone to become physically sick during the ceremony or the reception. With luck, you can get a member of the wedding party to do this.

7. Use many additives in the groom-mark's drinks during the prenuptial bachelor party.

8. Hire someone to slowly and dramatically flash the minister from the back of the church while everyone else is facing front. This also works well if there is a singer in the choir balcony. Try to upset him or her during a song.

9. Call the state police or the drug-enforcement people and give them a complete description of the car that will carry the bridal couple on the honeymoon. Report that the couple and the car are really dope mules, that is, couriers of the drug trade.

Media

The mass media—newspapers, radio, television, and magazines—can be helpful tools in getting even, or they can be your mark in a dirty trick. I suggest you keep your media-as-tool aspect relegated to local events and local media. In general, newspapers tend to be conservative and stodgy and not much interested in your rousing of the rabble. Most newspaper officials play golf with corporate officials, and their common bonds are advertising and profits.

Television likes good, visual consumer stories, and local TV stations will go for local controversy more often than will local newspapers. Here are some basic suggestions for using the media to help you in your getting-even campaigns.

If the editor says the event is news, then it goes out to the public as news. People don't make news; editors make news.

To impress editors you have to keep coming up with fresh action. You have to be visual, outrageous, funny, controversial, and brief. Your message has to be catchy, visual, and packaged to fit ninety seconds of time in the six- or eleven-o'clock news slot. It's no wonder long-winded academics end up with "Viewpoint," or "Talk Out" at 3:00 o'clock Monday morning. They don't know how to use TV.

Now, how do you get even with the media when they deserve it? There are several things you can do:

• Take or phone in a fake wedding story, being sure to give them a legitimate-looking bride-groom photo. It doesn't matter who the people in the picture really are. Most smaller and medium-sized papers will publish without checking, which could lead to all sorts of wonderful things if you've been inventive in your choice of marriage partners.

• Use a low-power mobile transmitter to add little bits of original programming to your community's commercial radio station. Some people did this in Syracuse, New York, and drove officials crazy with hilariously obscene fake commercials, news bulletins, etc.

• Newspapers often have huge rolls of newsprint in relatively unsecured storage areas. It is a low-risk mission to insert paper-destroying insects or chemicals into those rolls.

• Some small radio stations are often loosely attended at night. Often, only the on-duty DJ is around, and even he will have to go to the can sometime. You might be able to wait until then or to have an accomplice distract that DJ while you place a prerecorded cassette with a message of your own choosing on the air.

• With smaller newspapers, it is sometimes easy to get phony stories and/or pictures published. Using your imagination, you can certainly cause a variety of grief for a variety of reasons. Be sure to match your cure with their crime.

According to media consultant Jed Billet, if you have a financially weak radio station in your area, you can often place ads for your mark over the telephone. Agreeing, Eugene Barnes recalls, "A couple of years ago, I wanted to get back at a doctor who'd really screwed up my family with some terrible behavior in a business dealing. So I designated him as my mark and had him 'open a pizza business.' I called the radio station and had them run a saturation campaign of twenty-five spots per day listing his name and home address and telephone number, plus all sorts of promotional gimmicks, like free delivery, free Coke, stuff like that. He had to have his telephone disconnected for a week. The station ran the ads for a day and a half before the doctor got them pulled. He had 'customers' off and on, though, for the next ten days."

Newspapers, magazines, radio, and TV are businesses, very concerned about their profit-and-loss statements. Sales, both of advertising and of audience for that advertising, are vital to the media. Knowing this, old media hand Ben Bulova has a scheme that works well most of the time.

"Most newspapers will start a subscription with a telephone call," Bulova says. "You call in and order a subscription in your mark's name and address."

The next step, Bulova explains, is to call the mark and, using the real circulation manager's name, tell him that you are with the circulation department of the newspaper and that they're going to give the mark a free trial subscription. That way, when the papers start to arrive, the mark thinks they're free. When the bill arrives, the mark will call the real circulation person. That conversation would be interesting to overhear.

Bulova says that this will work with magazines and trade publications, as well. He advocates an entire string of such gifts.

Medical

Either steal real medical test-report forms from a hospital, clinic, or laboratory or have friend get them for you. If this doesn't work, a trusted printer will make some for you. You will also need matching return-address business envelopes to mail the reports to your mark. Get some technical advice from a medical textbook or a very trusted friend with a medical background, then prepare a series of embarrassing lab reports for your mark. This could include positive identification of such problems as venereal disease, drug dependence, cancer, yeast infection, or mental illness.

The mailing of the bogus report must be coordinated with a telephone call to the mark's spouse, employer, parents, parole officer, etc. Doctor Milo Weir, who helped with this idea, recommends that multiple copies of the diagnostic reports be sent to various other people. For example, a venereal-disease report copy could be sent to public-health officials, and a drug-problem report might go to the state narcotics bureau.

If you're waiting in a doctor's examining room you will probably see all sorts of goodies stacked around—syringes, common drugs, medical equipment, maybe a diploma or two. A couple of Yippies said they used to make appointments complaining of vague symptoms just so they could rip off goodies. Beyond simple pilferage, the opportunity exists here for introducing additives to various products.

This should tickle the fancy of those true sadists among you. It comes from the Olde Medical Almanak of Doctor Jerrold Andurson. He removes some of the Preparation H from the regular container and refills that with tabasco sauce. Andurson guarantees that this will give your hemorrhoidal mark one of the hottest seats she/he could feel.

Andurson adds, "That reminds me of the observation made by the man who caught his genitalia in a bear trap. He said that the second worst pain in his life came when he came to the end of the trap's chain."

One summer, Will Gressle had the misfortune to be incarcerated in a hospital wing run by a nurse who made Doctor Josef Mengele seem like Santa Claus. An easygoing sort, Gressle was driven to revenge by this nasty Brigadier of the Bedpans. Here's what he did about it.

"In late November I was visiting my uncle's ranch in Idaho, where he raises a few sheep. I got about seven pounds of farm-fresh sheep droppings and put it carefully in an opaque, airtight plastic sack," he relates.

"I put that in a box, wrapped it in bright Christmas paper, and stuck little happy-face and Christmas decals all over it. Then I wrapped all that in heavy brown paper and mailed it to the nurse, in care of the hospital. I put a fake return address on the package and a few holiday stickers on the outside, too.

"I'm sure the parcel arrived at the hospital, where they have a little tree in each wing and a small exchange of presents. It is my sincere hope that Nurse Nasty unwrapped my gift in front of a lot of nurses, doctors, and patients. She would finally get to the bag of sheep shit and a little note, which read, 'Just returning a tiny little bit of what you are so fond of dishing out in great amount,' signed, 'A Former Inmate.' "

Considering that the major side effect of medical treatment these days is terminal bankruptcy, it is little wonder that medical institutions and personnel have become the target of so much getting-even thinking. In speaking with people on both sides of this fight, I have concluded that there are only limited stunts you can direct against these specific targets. Yet the range of regular stunts presented in a dozen other chapters of this book are as effective against medical institutions and people as against any other subject—perhaps more so, given the self-held exalted status of the medical community.

For example, it's one thing if your mark is a contractor and suffers from a venereal disease because of your getting even—but think how it would work for a doctor! Gossip travels fast in the medical corridors.

However, if you are thirsting for a few little goodies to toss at the medical community, here's a mini-list of suggestions:

- Leave dead vermin at strategic points of a particular medical facility—near the coffee shop, the kitchen, the emergency room, the visitors' lounge, etc.
- Dressed in whites or other appropriate uniform, slip in with cafeteria or kitchen help and put some harmless food coloring into foods. Or if you can get in to where the staff food is prepared, more powerful additives may be used.
- Borrow some medical-insurance identification from a cooperative friend or otherwise obtain someone else's identification. Use this to charge medical bills, either real or imaginary. The point is to get bills sent to a totally innocent or totally unaware third party. If it's your friend, he or she is part of the scam and will pretend to be outraged about the whole business. Either way, the medical facility is the real mark.

Military

The canard that began World War II in Europe was based on the tenets of dirty trickery. On 1 September 1939, a group of what appeared to be Polish soldiers attacked a German radio station near the two countries' borders. In "self-defense," German units then fired upon Polish units in Danzig.

That stunt actually started World War II.

The so-called aggressors who attacked the German radio station were actually inmates from German concentration camps, dressed in Polish army uniforms, driven from Germany to the radio site near the border and injected with the lethal drug skophedal. The dying men were spread out in what appeared to be a firefight scenario and riddled with bullets by German SS men. A few who survived told the story. The German code name for this "military" operation was Canned Goods.

While serving as a guest of Uncle Sam, I had some intelligence assignments. There I found out that there are two types of intelligence—military and human. Or as Groucho Marx said, "Military intelligence is a contradiction in terms."

You can get arrested for falsely wearing the real uniform of the armed forces. That's why some tricksters don't wear an actual uniform but either build or rent a replica that surely looks real. That way they are free to give speeches, shout orders, make bogus policy pronouncements, hold press conferences, use rank, and all sorts of other bits of theater from which the average citizen might infer that the actor really does represent the official military. This sort of incorrect inference could cause all sorts of public-relations and worse problems for the military establishment. Could this be considered contributing to the delinquency of a major?

Although the Yippies are a generation or so forgotten, and at least as this is written, our army is no longer a high-profile domestic villain, someone may still want to pull one off for old times' sake. A Jerry Rubin trick would be to find a somewhat deserted area of a large public recreational park. Place some official-looking, commercially printed signs in prominent places. The signs will say:

WARNING

Army war dogs training in this area. Very dangerous. Keep all children and pets within sight. If Army dog approaches do not move under any circumstances.

—U.S. Army. Official—

Guess who will get blamed when frightened citizens complain to the town, city, county, state, feds, or whoever is in charge of the park. Guess how many brass hats will have to visit the site, investigate, write reports, and give explanations.

According to Captain DeGeorge Media, things got pretty bizarre over at the Pentagon when the intelligence boys found that OPEC intelligence agents had broken the Pentagon ZIP code. Hah! Can you military agents reading this book break the code I just used? — MESSAGE ENDS—

Speaking of military-intelligence agents, I recall that especially obnoxious recruits, second lieutenants, and other lower-order sorts could often be sent on a fool's errand that often multiplied into more harassment than the stunt was really worth. If your mark caught a first sergeant with an especially bad hangover or an ill-tempered senior officer who'd just discovered that his daughter was pregnant by some recruit from a Third World military unit attached for training—well, you get the idea. Anyhow, you can send these marks out to bring back a rubber flag to be flown on rainy days. Or you can send the idiot out to bring back the cannon report. If you're air force, a five-gallon drum of prop wash is an appropriate errand target—or a bucket of prop pitch or a box of RPMs. The navy is good for sending someone to get stuffing for the crow's nest, a biscuit gun for the galley, etc. You can always send someone to the post or ship's print shop for some dotted ink. A trip to the supply stores for plaid paint is fun. The best part is that they almost always fall for such nonsense. I think that says something about the military's effect on human thought processes.

If you have access to the sound system over which Reveille is played each morning, you might move up that magic time of day by, oh, say half an hour or forty-five minutes—just enough to screw things up. The next day, make it fifteen minutes late. Another day, play it in the middle of the night. Always play it a bit louder than usual.

In a similar sense, at one summer camp, a national guardsman switched the Reveille record for a rock record one morning. Another morning, recorded Rusty Warren and her humor greeted the troops.

Some solid general advice for getting even within the military comes from a high-ranking and experienced military man who is now a biggie in the VFW. You know he's qualified to give advice.

He suggests, "The military is a blizzard of paper, paranoia, and intrigue. A dirty trickster who understands this and can parody the system will drive a mark to ruin. A good primer for action is to read *Catch 22.*

"You will find an abundance of politics, ass kissing, back biting, gossip, and reputation hunting and destroying among career military people. It's an absolutely fertile ground to grow dirty tricks. A nastily clever person will have no trouble getting even for all the petty bullshit the military inflicts upon sensitive and logical people."

Thinking about sensitive and logical people brought Selective Service to mind. When we last had a draft, during the Vietnam unpleasantness, all sorts of young men did all sorts of bizarre things to evade it. However, a true dirty trickster would think in 180 degree terms—why not invade the draft? Simply register yourself in about three dozen locations with an equal number of draft boards. As far as I know, the law came down on only you if you failed to register. I guess I don't have to list the reasons why someone might wish to get even with the Selective Service system or a particular board.

Motion Pictures

Hugh Troy was a famed artist who was also a hardcore practical joker. Once, the manager of a motion-picture theater offended Troy. Troy went into the same theater the next evening, after secreting several jars of huge moths on his person. Soon after the feature began, he released the creatures, all of which flew directly into the beam of the projector and stayed and stayed and stayed. . . .

Have you ever sat down in a darkened theater, later finding your posterior has been parked on someone else's sticky candy bar or chewing gum from the last show? Did you ever go to a movie house, feel you were ripped off by the poor feature, get up and leave well before the film is finished, and still be unable to get even a partial refund?

Peanuts Campbell used the restroom of a local movie house, and when he flushed the facility it backfired on him, staining his new pants and causing other patrons to both turn up their noses and turn away their eyes in annoyance.

Another patron was served buttered popcorn in a tub that leaked the gooey liquid all over his date's dress. Management refused to pay any claims. The patron of a stage theater had his pants torn on a protruding seat spring. No damages were paid, and his attorney said the amount was too small to take to court.

What next? Peanuts Campbell has an answer.

You must have a quick, clear exit after this action. Peanuts Campbell used to take a container of lukewarm vegetable soup into a movie theater. He sat in the front row of the balcony. He made the sounds of being sick to his stomach—choking, coughing, retching—then dumped the soup on the people below. The same tactic also works at sporting events, public meetings—anywhere there is a crowd below you. But you must have a good escape plan.

The point of all this is to have dozens of irate patrons demanding damage settlements from the management of the establishment. If you don't feel adventuresome enough to dump on your fellow customers, simply go into the theater early and, while no one else is around, place gooey chewing gum on random seats. Or pour your soup on some random seats. Pick seats away from an aisle or ceiling safety lights. You may also use a slow-drying glue on the seats.

Municipal
Services

A former CIA operative who specialized in sabotage shared a couple of theoretical ideas about some cheap tricks. He suggests that if a municipality has corroded you with its parking corruption, then a return is only fair. He suggests a squirt or two of concentrated battery acid into a parking-meter slot. Repeat as necessary, he adds.

He has an excellent caveat to go with this, though: "If you do this sort of thing needlessly and unprovoked, it is nothing more than criminal vandalism, which is stupid, and you deserve what you get if you're caught.

"But, if you're doing it as a justified retaliation for something unjustified which was done to you and for which you have no other recourse, then give it your best shot."

You can also put epoxy or similar glue into that parking-meter slot, but that is readily visible. Another idea, according to Billy Bellan, is to screw up the meter so that it might still accept a few more coins but not operate any more. That way, more citizens get tickets because of an inoperable meter. There is more fuss and confusion for the authorities this way. He suggests that small washers coated with liquid solder or glue be placed in the meter slot.

A few sawhorses and some official-looking signs can close down a busy road. Set them up just before rush hour, and you will create chaos. If you do it well, it will be an hour before the mess is settled and things are back to semi-normal.

You know how public-employee unions are? Call the head of one union or some shop steward in your city or county. Say you are some big honcho—like a commissioner or a councilperson. Just raise royal hell. Get personal and abusive about some issue that's in the news. Try to provoke the person you are talking to. Faced with the call later, the official will honestly deny everything. Given the state of management-union relations at the moment, I doubt that many union folks will believe the management person you impersonated.

If the union is your mark, pick up some identification—credit cards, fake license, or something else that would document that you are the selected union official. Go to some municipal facility and pull off one of the dirty tricks mentioned in this book. On your way out, "accidentally" drop your mark's ID at the scene.

Never turn in false fire alarms. Fire is a serious business, and most firemen are volunteers who do a helluva job protecting you and the rest of your community. I have a lot of respect for firemen. Don't mess with them or their functions.

Usually, this is true of police, too, unless you happen to run into neo-Nazi stormtroopers on the force. For some reason police work can attract the town bully. Maybe it's the guns, uniforms, saps, and the power of the badge that draw them in. But as any good cop will tell you—they get more than their share of hoods.

It's cool to screw up the hoods in uniform. But stay off the cases of the good cops. They are decent people with tough enough jobs. The life of a cop is a hundred times tougher in many ways than your job. Stick to selective targeting here.

If you do have a badass cop or two it might be fun to chain the afflicted black-and-white to the car parked behind it or to something that will cause damage, à la the film *American Graffiti,* while the law persons are having a coffee break.

Another tactic involves the use of the pay telephone. Call the parents of kids who get into trouble and threaten the hell out of them and their kids. You will identify yourself as Officer Hitler, or whatever name the bad cop goes by.

You could have the officer call women late at night. Call both single and married women. Sound drunk, play the radio as if the officer is in a bar. Tell the woman you saw her, fell in love, and used official records to find out her name and telephone number. Tell her you are a far better lover than she's ever had. Get graphic. Praise her anatomy specifically. Be boastful. Make demands. Make officially backed demands. If someone else, like a husband, lover, or friend, comes on the line, be abusive and drunkenly threatening. This works best if you happen to know that the cop is drinking in a local bar as you make the few calls. You might mention the name of the bar. This trick does not have to be limited to cops, but it works better that way.

Neighborhoods

Be the first in your mark's neighborhood to become a blockbuster. It's time to fuss up the mark's neighbors again. Find a real estate agency that deals mostly with blacks or Chicanos. Posing as the mark, call the agency and invite a salesperson out to talk about the sale of the mark's *neighbor's* house. Don't hoke up your role with a lot of brotherhood stuff—play it straight. Now, if the mark is a good, solid white citizen living in a neighborhood of same-minded bigots, you have a wonderful deal going for you. The kicker is, you give the salesman the mark's name and the neighbor's address. Obviously, you must pick the most rednecked, bigoted neighbor to be the fall guy for the black or Chicano salesperson. By the time the "mistake" gets straightened out who's going to believe the mark? Not only have you alienated his neighbor, but you have taken a big chunk out of his credibility and popularity. Black is beautiful, especially when it's the color of the mark's reputation among his peers.

This stunt works—a person I know used it. He's a professional ball player who went into a furniture store with his wife to buy a living-room-and-den suite of furniture. The clerk was bigoted and exceptionally nasty. My friend calmly asked to see the manager, who turned out to be worse than the clerk. The black customer suddenly flashed his wallet full of green money, and both white guys blanched. No further words were exchanged as the married couple left the store. Two days later my friend called a black real estate agency. You just read about what happened next.

Richard M. Nixon

Richard Nixon has all the charm and warmth of an obscene Christmas card. Let's remember him always. For instance, whenever you are asked for your Social Security number for no good purpose to you, and when giving a false one will not harm you, give them Richard Nixon's number. It's the least we can do for all that he did to us. Richard M. Nixon's Social Security number is 567-68-0515.

Notary Seal

Possession of or access to a notary seal is vital to a trickster. To the average layperson and common lawyer, the mere fact of a notary seal on a document is like God's own rubber stamp. Many times you will need to have a document notarized as part of the scams explained in this book. Having your own seal kit is the obvious answer. Some firms sell real ones—"official"—on the black market. Some sell replica kits, which are not official. Avoid these—some are so crude that they wouldn't even fool a politician. I know one trickster who had a seal kit custom made—by a con in a California prison print shop. The con had been an engraver in civilian life and really knew his work.

You can buy a blank die kit openly from any shop stocking seals. Corporations use them all the time, which may give you a tip right there about the value of seals. You can have a custom seal made by many of these companies.

However you obtain it, get a notary-seal kit. The uses of it pay it off the first few times you scam someone. In addition to the notary seal, you should also get a couple of other official-looking dies. Commercially and openly, you can obtain blank dies with state logos, or you can get one that looks like a U.S. eagle. All sorts of possibilities exist here.

Oil Companies

The soaring oil prices and lack of leadership got so bad late in 1979 that all the dedicated and honest congresspersons got together to protest big oil. But who is afraid of seven people!

You remember the Great Gasoline Ripoff of 1979, when the oil companies raped the driving public both coming and going? Petroleum magnate Jimmy Slushslinger related this story: A regular customer pulled up to a service station and said, "Fill 'er up." As he was paying his bill, he said, "Oh gosh, all I have is a fifty-dollar bill. Sorry."

The gas jockey replied, "No problem—you can pay me the rest next week."

Starting rumors at the inappropriate time is the something else to do. For example, if your mark happens to be a gasoline station owned by a major company, and a lot of citizens are in a gas line waiting for their semi-annual pittance of overpriced petroleum, you could walk onto the scene wearing oil-smeared coveralls and stroll down the line—just out of signt of the real station personnel. Tell parked motorists that all fuel is gone. If anyone gets belligerent, use the "I'm just a minimum-wage employee, but the boss said if anyone got angry to send the bastard to him, because he'll sure cool him off in a hurry." Don't wait around for the cooling-off period.

Cut out a stencil that has the word ARAMCO on it, then

spray it with white paint under the word STOP on all the stop signs in your town or near a large oil-company office building or refinery. Aramco, in case you didn't know, is the major oil cartel that works with OPEC to rob American citizens.

During the 1979 oil-company blitzkrieg against the American public, a guerrilla fighter hit back. He cut a sliding door in the floor of his van. He had a three-hundred-gallon tank installed in the van, along with a small electrically operated pump and a twenty-foot hose. He drove in only to company-owned gasoline stations, parked over the main tank caps, then used a wrench to open one. He dipped in his hose, turned on the quiet pump, and filled his tank with three-hundred gallons of free tigers.

Bruno Tannetto dislikes oil companies. For years he played credit-card bingo with them, pirated cards, counterfeited cards, and ran up huge debts and skipped them—all in the name of guerrilla warfare against the oil giants. He also saved all the postage-paid return envelopes they used to include with his bills. Since he rarely paid, he had quite a collection of envelopes, which is when he really got his rocks off.

Bruno collected a bunch of heavy rocks and boxed them up in a sturdy carton, which he marked, "Caution—Geological-Core Samples" and addressed to whatever oil company he had the envelopes for. Using the envelope as the "postage," he mailed this heavy box first class to the oil company, which had to spring for the huge postal charges. He did this many times to several of the giants.

Giggi Hilliard tells about a chap who played nasty to get an oil-company operation into some difficulty. The agent provocateur's mode was forgery, and here's what he did. While on a routine visit to the oil company's corporate offices, he swiped an internal memo from a desk while the secretary was out of the room. He had his printer create some blank memo sheets using the company logo. Then, using a safe IBM typewriter and following the style of the company original, the trickster wrote a very sensitive memo from one oil-company manager to another. The memo discussed the need for deep cover to prevent leakage of sensitive financial contributions to state and national political officials. He then leaked the memo to the press.

"The idea behind this," Hilliard explains, "is to cause the oil company, or whatever mark you choose, to have to explain and deny. Nobody believes them anyhow, so you give that big business another credibility black eye. Great, huh? You can use this same tactic with any corporation, utility, or business. The list of sensitive topics is limitless. But always use real officials' names on the forgeries."

Consult *Overthrow* (see section on Ma Bell) to obtain the telephone-credit-card numbers for the major oil companies. Use this information to your best advantage. Beware: Oil companies hire experienced FBI, CIA, and drug-enforcement people for their security staffs. The security and intelligence operations of the oil industry are as nasty and as effective as anything the feds could put together, and they are not hindered with what few laws do restrict the federal law-enforcement people. You have no civil or human rights when the oil-company security and intelligence people go after you. When dirty tricking the oil companies it is crucial that you practice WYA, which means Watch Your Ass!

Recently, a lady trickster called the wife of an oil-company robber baron and pretended to be a lowly cleaning lady at corporate headquarters. Telling Mrs. Oil Executive that she, the cleaning lady, was a good Christian lady who believed in the God-given sanctity of family and marriage, our "cleaning lady" revealed that she often had to clean fresh semen stains from the couch in Mr. Executive's office after "private, after-hours conferences" between the boss and his young secretary. That's all, just a simple telephone call from a simple, honest, God-fearing lady to a stay-at-home wife who's probably already paranoid about her executive-husband's extracurricular sex life. If more right-minded citizens cared about the moral decline among executives in the oil industry . . .

By now you surely owe that friendly and cooperative printer a few glasses of lemonade for being your co-conspirator in a number of scams. Here's one more. Many of your area's prominent citizens should receive a fancy invitation to attend a special local social function hosted by your favorite oil corporation. The invitation should read something like this: "Admit bearer and guest for the special Hollywood entertainment and buffet on [day and date]. Informal dress from [time] to [time] at [location]."

Try to pick a Saturday or Sunday and mail the invitation only a day or so prior to the nonevent. This won't give the doubters, cynics, press, or anyone else much time to ascertain the veracity of the invitation.

In the summer of 1979, after reading newspaper stories about how the major oil companies were raking in untaxed windfall profits ranging from 35 to 130 percent, Melvin Lierd decided enough was enough.

"I had no mere dirty tricks in mind; my whole idea was to rip those bastards as much as I could, the greedy, lying thieves," Melvin muttered mildly.

His plan was simple. He obtained credit cards from as many companies as possible and charged as many products and services as possible *only from company-owned stations.*

"I ran up bills as high and as fast as possible. I had absolutely no intention of paying," Melvin explained.

Asked if he got the cards in his own name, Melvin responded, "Nah, I got them in a fake company name. I run up as much as I can, then pay them each $5 or so, claiming it is only a token payment because we're a new company, but I will make the rest soon, blah, blah, blah.

"The greedy bastards are so anxious to make money they'll just add on those outrageous interest charges—usury rates, they are—and drool at how much they're screwing me on financing.

"I'll string them along for a couple months; then, if they get serious, I'll simply dissolve my company and let them eat their bills."

Do lawsuits bother Melvin? He rates lawyers and judges slightly below clam feces on his scale of respect, and he says, "Let them sue the company. It has no assets. Plus, they gotta find me. Let me tell you something, old son— you have to use the law. There is no justice, so you use the law to suit yourself. How do you suppose the big oil companies and the big lawyers and the big judges and all the other crooked snakes got so powerful—by using the law!"

At last report, Melvin Lierd was draining the oil giants at a rate far in excess of his own expectations. He has invited many of you to join him.

Not content to live by the rule of "steal from them before they steal from you," Carl Bepp likes to *add* things to the oil-company stations' bulk tanks. He says that many of the additives described earlier in this book and elsewhere will work. But, he does have a sentimental favorite.

"Once, some land rapists were drilling a noisy, sloppy gas well near the home of a friend of mine," he relates. "Since they were stealing from the land, I decided to steal some land from them.

"One evening, when they were finished drilling for the day, I got some of that slimy, mucky gunk that the drillers had bailed out of the well. I took it to my most-hated oil company's very own station and dumped three two-gallon buckets of that gunk down into their bulk tanks."

He said he has also used several gallons of refurbished solid wastes, known as sludge, as another additive for the oil-company products.

Party Time

It's always fun to drop into a number of what I call olde phart bars—the seedy downtown places where drunken old men hang around from morning to evening, pouring down oceans of booze but never seeming to get falling-down drunk. The place stinks, and they stink. It's a great place to make up a guest list for your mark's party.

Have a couple of beers and talk with the old duffers, unless everyone's uptight about a stranger being there. Usually, though, old pharts in bars are friendly. After a bit of social ice has been clinked, tell them about a keg party "you're" having. Obviously, you use the mark's name and give his address. Early Sunday afternoon is a good time to schedule the party.

If you hit enough bars on Saturday and talk to enough old drunks, your mark should have a helluva wingding show up at the house Sunday afternoon, all hung over and roaring to get started again. *Salud!*

Remember Donald Segretti, Richard Nixon's unofficial classless clown? Apparently, he could have easily written this book from memory. In any case, Segretti came up with a party "on behalf of" the late Hubert Humphrey, thought to be a threat to Nixon back in 1972. Segretti printed up thousands of invitations to a luncheon with Humphrey, set for 1 April in Milwaukee. He had the invitations distributed all over the black ghettos of that city.

They read, "FREE!—All you can eat—lunch with beer, wine or soda. With Senator Hubert H. Humphrey, Lorne Greene, Mrs. Martin Luther King." He gave a time and place, too. Of course, there was no lunch, no drinks, and no people there other than hundreds of hungry, thirsty, and highly irritated people. Should we say they were non-Humphrey voters?

The next stunt demands that you or your personal agent arrive at a party thrown by the mark. Among your mark's other munchie dishes you should include a selection of candied laxatives. You can serve a commercial product, which is already adequately disguised as candy, or you can make your own by coating and/or coloring stronger constipation-relief medicines. Be creative with the disguise. The result of having people eat mittfuls of these bowel busters is breathtaking.

Woolsey Newcomer and Enos Pomerene remember a party a number of years back in which a barrel of beer washed down the thirst of the folks gobbling bogus candy, which was really a powerful laxative.

"The digestive hell began the morning after the party and lasted up to four days for some people," Woolsey recalled. "The guys had been stuffing those laxatives in their mouths and washing it all down with draft beer. What a combination! We had some sick folks."

Woolsey always wondered who had infiltrated the candy dish.

A more subtle relation to the dish full of laxatives is to get a candy mold from a confectionery-supply house. These are usually in the form of little animals, Santas, etc. Molds for chocolate Easter bunnies are probably the most common example. You simply melt a little bit of real chocolate and a good bit of chocolate laxative together, fill the mold, and turn out some homemade candy with an explosive punch to it.

Finally, if you know your mark is having a party any

given day or night, that would be a splendid time to cause the utilities to be shut off or otherwise disrupted. Contemporary civilized socializers just can't handle disruption of modern conveniences like power and water, and they tend to remember the host/hostess (your mark) and identify him/her with the failure. It's a good, subtle, nasty trick.

Pen Pals

Men are fools when it comes to being conned by the game that preceded even prostitution. For example, if you could create a fictional lady, she could be as seductive as you wanted her to be. After all, to the mark she is an image brought on by the words you put down on paper or maybe use on the telephone. You want him to become her pen pal.

As this scam progresses, you hope the emphasis will turn to personal matters. It's even more fun if the mark is married, because then he'll make a bigger ass of himself. Your fictional pen-pal lady must build a desire in the mark, by doing just what comes so naturally.

The climax is an assignation setup in an exotic city as far away as reality will allow. Setting up this sting calls for teasing creativity and all sorts of façades like flowers, hints of gifts, Frederick's of Hollywood apparel, bogus sexy Polaroids, etc.

The next to last thing you will do in this stunt is discontinue your post-office box or whatever mail-drop address you were using for his return messages. The last thing you will do is mail, call, or telegraph this final message, "Meet you at the Sin City Hotel, suite 625, tonight at 10 P.M. I'll have the tub and me all warm and wet."

Naturally, only one of you will arrive, and he'll hardly be in the mood to start without "you."

Personal

You can easily turn your mark into a fabled thief, according to former private detective Trowbridge Bannister. You need a full-face photo of your mark, plus a furtive longer shot of the type usually taken by surveillance cameras. Take these pictures and your WARNING copy to a trusted printer to get some posters made.

Bannister explains: "You make up posters warning merchants and customers to be on the lookout for the mark. Display his name and picture on the poster in a prominent location, along with the big headlines about this person's being a thief, shoplifter, or pickpocket. A small amount of copy could explain some brief history of your mark's criminal career. Make it sound realistic—don't get cute. Sign the thing by the local community's merchants association or something like that."

Bannister says the final step is for you to take these posters to various stores and carefully post them around the stores. Avoid being seen. Doing this in a large shopping mall or in a busy downtown area ensures that thousands of local citizens will get your message about the mark.

You could also use the same tactic and mark your mark as a sex offender, child molester, or worse . . . a pornographer.

You can write horrible "news" stories about your mark and have your printer set them in newspaper style, complete with column-length lines and, perhaps, border rules and datelines. You should make the dateline a town in which your mark formerly lived. In these bogus news stories, she/he could be the subject of almost any sort of execrable activity, such as child molesting, sexual perversion, child abuse, killing kittens, starving and beating puppies, poaching fawns, self abuse in public, and on and on.

Naturally, the more authentic you make the story, the better the scam will go when you send Xerox copies to the mark's employer, family, and friends. Have your mail postmarked from the mark's former city and include a short note from "a friend who thinks you ought to know the truth."

During World War II, the British SOE made use of a harassing substance that became known as "Who, Me?" It was later adopted by the American OSS. Essentially, it was a tube of obnoxious-smelling liquid that would be squirted onto an enemy's clothing or body during some time that would not cause alarm, such as while she or he was sleeping or bathing, or during the jostling of a crowd. Exposed to the air, the liquid immediately gave off the pungent odor of strong, fresh human feces.

The product was manufactured by Federal Laboratories near Pittsburgh under an OSS contract. It proved quite satisfactory and, as it was packaged, a user could eject one cubic centimeter of Who, Me? as a thin liquid stream at distances up to ten feet. There was little danger of self contamination if it was handled properly.

According to OSS records, two different formulas were used—a fecal odor for the European theater and a "skunky/body" odor for the Pacific theater. The research-backed reasoning is that because the Japanese often used human wastes as agricultural fertilizers, they would not be as sensitive to the odor as the Germans. Both forms were found to be "noticeably lasting for well over a day, despite frequent washings."

You probably want to know if you can buy surplus Who, Me? from your local army-navy outlet. No, but you can produce it yourself using the following formula:

919 g. mineral white oil
20 g. skatol
20 g. n-butyric acid
20 g. n-valeric acid
20 g. n-caproic acid
1 g. amyl mercaptan

That will produce a kilogram of the fecal-smelling liquid. You could alter the amounts to produce as much or as little as you think you'll need. If you prefer the skunky odor, here's the formula on a relative-percentage basis:

65 percent mineral white oil
10 percent butyric acid
10 percent mercaptan
15 percent alpha ionone

Another great pretender to aroma of woodpussy is 3-methyl-1-butane-thiol. It is easily obtainable in chemical-supply stores and smells almost as terrible as the real thing.

If you are assertive enough to get the chemicals and mix up a batch of composition, you probably already have the applicator selected and don't need further help. If not, use this as a lesson in becoming more self-sufficient. Happy squirting.

If you're too insecure to become a home chemist, you could obtain some formaldehyde, which is popularly known as embalming fluid. This stuff is bad news. It stinks and can burn your skin. According to some folks, if enough of it gets into the air it will vaporize. If this takes place in a room, that room will be cleared of all breathing objects for several hours.

Being a liquid, formaldehyde may be squirted from any appropriate applicator. It is fairly devastating stuff, but you can get it in small amounts if you are involved in biological or chemical experiments. Sometimes, a white lab coat makes a good cover when you go shopping in a drugstore or medical-supply house outside your neighborhood or town.

A bit more personal, but nowhere near as dangerous, is to dip your fingers in warm water, come up behind your mark, and as you deliver an ear-shattering sneeze, fling the water on the mark's neck or back. This works well with backless dresses, at the pool, or almost anywhere, for that matter. Escape may be a vital concern here, depending on your mark's sense of humor.

If your mark is one or both members of a young couple, Dana Bearpaw had a policy of calling the parents of one or both. Playing the role of an older, irate neighbor, he would shout, "Look, I don't care how much [description of carnal activity to be left up to the discretion of the caller] your son/daughter engages in with every male/female/ whatever every damn night. Just keep them out of our backyard when they're doing it. If you're any kind of a parent you'll talk to them about all this."

Parents usually take this sort of thing to heart . . . which causes all sorts of communication and credibility problems with their youngsters.

If you want to endear your mark to his/her neighbors, go to the local public library and consult the street-address or cross-reference city directory to learn who your mark's neighbors are and their phone numbers. If you can't find such a directory in a more rural area, just drive and list names from mailboxes.

Later, call some selected neighbors using your mark's name and be sure you identify yourself as a close neighbor. Then, launch into something like, "I want to come over and talk to you about [Communism, homosexuality, child pornography, drug legalization, busing, or whatever]. I want you to sign a petition demanding fair treatment under the law for [whatever topic you've chosen]."

Be pushy and really work to make your mark's reputation a deserved one.

Many times women are certain their men are out somewhere adding significantly to the statistical rate for sexual infidelity. When one lady had absolute proof of her man's bombastic bedding habits with other ladies, she devised a scheme that would guarantee his sticking around. On one rare night when he was in their bed, his mate waited until he had fallen into his usual deep sleep, then gently applied one of the new superglue products to both his penis and his leg and held the two together for the short bonding time so well advertised on television.

No elephant, tractor, or pro footballer could break that bond. It took the delicate skill of the family physician to make the separation, a move matched that afternoon by the vindicated lady, who also cut out on her very sore ex-man.

Photography

Ask any competent photographer who also has some sense of humor, about composite photographs. They're easy to make—the tabloids used them for years. It's a photo where someone has been added to a group, someone's face has been used on the body of another person, or an entirely new photograph is created simply by using composite parts.

This is a very useful dirty trick and one that bears the stamp of approval of the CIA and the FBI.

Unless you're competent in photography, including copying, darkroom technique, and minor retouching and airbrushing, or unless you have a very trusted friend who will help you, you'd best forget this one. However, done well, the uses of composites are limited only by your imagination. Here are some examples passed along by some of the sources of this book:

• A "photo" showing the mark leaving a motel room with a person of the opposite sex.

• A "photo" sent anonymously to the police showing the mark or the mark's vehicle engaged in some illegal activity—like poaching, dealing drugs, or corrupting the morals of minors. Be sure the license number of the vehicle is visible.

• A "photo" showing the mark's spouse nude and in a

compromising pose with a companion—human, animal, or whatever.

● A "photo" showing the mark in a compromising situation with a person of the same sex could be sent to the mark's employer. This will surely mark your mark a gay who will live in infamy.

Like other topical areas in this book, this one is strictly a technical suggestion. You will have to furnish the motive, rationale, and application for your own photographic nastiness.

Pornography

Buy some really sleazy skin magazines—ones featuring kiddie porn, animals, etc. Use an IBM typewriter and some pressure-sensitive mailing labels to prepare phony address labels in your mark's name. Place them on the porno magazines. You can start by leaving a few magazines in doctors' or dentists' waiting rooms, Sunday-school reading rooms, and the periodical shelves of your local library. The public will think your mark is passing along his used literature.

You might also get some paste-over copyright stickers printed with your mark's name and address. Buy some raunchy porno, put the stickers in somewhere on the title area, then take the goods to local grade school and junior high school areas and sell them to the children. Do this only once. If you do get caught, *swear* the mark paid you to distribute his pornography.

This tactic is best used against bluenose censors and others who would impose their own personal beliefs upon you under penalty of law. According to civil libertarian Townsend McFerrick, this piece of counter-propaganda is almost always effective against the personal outrages of puritanical dictators.

Politics

As public jesters from Jerry Rubin to Jerry Ford to Hunter Thompson to Frank Rizzo to Nobody have discovered, any fool with twenty-five dollars and twenty-five signatures can run for public office. As Rubin asks, "What better way to make fun of the political system than to run for public office?"

He's right. It gives you a legal platform to attack and ridicule the institutions and people who deserve such attention. If you have either sophisticated or totally rustic local media, and know how to manage and manipulate media people, you will get oodles of free publicity. That isn't very difficult, as many people demonstrate daily.

Neil Mothra, who understands politicians, came up with this stunt. If your mark is a candidate or political VIP, if his coterie doesn't know you, and if it's a very hot, shirtsleeve day, you're all set. Slip into the meeting or reception area, walk briskly up to the mark, and offer politely, "May I take your coat, sir?" The impression is that you are going to hang it up for him. It will be best if you are dressed up or in some form of institutional-looking uniform. You simply take the coat away with you. If you also have the person's wallet, you must do what you think is best and most honest to all concerned.

One of the grandest tricks of all time happened in 1960, when a beaming crook named Richard Nixon was posing in San Francisco's Chinatown with a group of Chinese youngsters holding a large banner spelling out a slogan in native characters. The photo ran locally and was picked up by both wire services and network television and disseminated to the entire nation.

The very next day, a worried staffer told candidate Nixon the Chinese banner had said, "What about the Hughes Loan?" It was a reference to the Howard Hughes cash payoff to Nixon's brother Donald, in the form of a "loan." At the same time, Nixon found out that thousands of fortune cookies had been passed out at the same rally, each containing the same message, this time in English: "Ask him about the Hughes Loan."

The antics of Donald Segretti, court jester to the Committee to ReElect the President (CREEP) in 1972, should fill your imagination with enough fertilizer to devise tactics of your own, should you wish to advise a political candidate.

For example, during the Florida primary, one of Segretti's raiders paid a young lady twenty dollars to streak naked outside Ed Muskie's hotel room, shouting, "I love Ed Muskie!" and "Father my child, Ed!" During a Muskie picnic, a Segretti trooper had a chemist mix up a batch of butyl percaptan, which is, as you know, a grossly foul, stinking mess. The after-action report to Segretti noted that among the guests, "everybody thought the food was bad."

If the bigshot candidate is having one of those hundred-dollar-a-plate fundraisers, your candidate should hold a ninety-nine-cent, blue-collar special—chipped-ham or bologna-and-cheese sandwiches. Blue paper plates and cups would contrast nicely with the power establishment's fancy eatery. The theme could be "Why pay a hundred dollars for bologna from [other candidate]?"

Here's some further nastiness at the expense of three marks—a politician, the Postal Service, and the the citizen you've chosen. You secure a franked postal envelope from your political mark. Carefully steam and remove the original mailing-address label. Using a rented or public IBM electric typewriter, carefully type in the name of your citizen mark on an IBM address label. Stick this label on the envelope.

The rest of this stunt depends on how nasty you are and how much revenge you feel you must squeeze from the mark(s). Some general suggestions for the contents of this envelope include: Heavily anti-Semitic propaganda for a Jewish mark; fanatical antireligious material for a religious sort; very explicit pornography for a very straight person; homemade Polaroid photos featuring closeups of dead pet animals—roadkills and mutilations—for sensitive animal lovers; Polaroid closeups of genitalia, both human and animal, for very proper people; and on and on.

Most marks will blame all this on the person whose return address is on the envelope—the political candidate.

Congressmen (there are rarely Congresswomen) have postal franking privileges that allow them a lot of free mail. A longtime politician baiter, Ted Shoemaker, decided to help a least-favored Congressman. Obtaining a franked envelope from his own mailbox, Shoemaker had a printer duplicate the postage-free envelope. By the way, this is a serious federal crime. He also prepared a mailing in which the ultraconservative congressman announced his backing for abortion and legalized marijuana, saying, "Times have changed, and we old farts have to change with them." Further, the letter had the politician saying, "You get drunk on booze—why not let the kids get high on pot? You cheat on your spouse—why not let the kids get a little free fun too?"

As you might imagine, the constituency was terminal Bible Belt. Shoemaker addressed, stuffed, and mailed a thousand of these messages, including copies to many media outlets. It took only two days for the old pol to claim fraud, but by that time the bogus letter had received lots of media attention, and more than a few old voters had made up their minds their good old boy was actually guilty of the whole thing anyway.

Shoemaker says, "He may have gotten some sympathetic backlash, though. This kind of thing can backfire, so be careful."

Barclay Skinner, the activist who championed women for membership in the National Jaycees, developed a frothing dislike for an especially weasel-like political candidate. This man's major credentials were that he'd served as a legal advisor for the Warren Commission, which tells you a lot about his lack of honor, intelligence, and integrity.

Skinner hired an actor who was a real lookalike for this politician and had the ringer travel the state giving speeches and press conferences in the real politician's name. The actor made all sorts of oddball, controversial, and asinine statements. He insulted local leaders, heroes, and institutions. He came off as a real sphincter.

Because the real politician was not really well-known either personally or visually, the impersonation worked well for the planned week. The real candidate found out about this and tried to stop it, but he was a week too late. He did not do well on election day. By that time, Skinner and his actor friend had faded back into the shrouded mists of heroic anonymity.

"Ah, politicians, God's unchosen people!" Skinner beamed.

Postal Service

M. J. Banks once sent her mother a Bible via the U.S. Postal Service. By the time it arrived, seven of the Ten Commandments were broken.

If you like your mail deliverer but dislike the U.S. Postal Service, Loren Eugene Sturgis has good news for you. He feels that ordinary citizens are already subsidizing the big corporations and their junk-mail advertising. He fights junk mail, which we'll get to in a moment. But, here is one of Loren's ways of cutting down on your own personal postal overhead.

Use Elmer's glue to coat the surface of stamps. This substance defeats the cancellation imprint enough that when you soak the stamp in lukewarm water, both the Elmer's and the cancellation ink come right off. Then you reglue the back of the stamp and use it again and again and again. This is a real money-saver for those who use a lot of postage, Loren points out. Your local postmaster would also point out how illegal this stunt is. Whom would you rather believe?

Rufus and Ruthie Luv are true rebels. Ruf used to work for the postal service, and he claims that automatic sorting machines really can't tell stamp denominations. For example, he said letters do go through with Easter Seals in place of stamps. He also suggests placing your stamp in the lower right corner. That way, the automatic canceling device will miss it and someone can reuse the stamp.

The U.S. Postal Service also furnishes you with games you can play with your mark. If you've ever moved, you know how happy USPS is to give you change-of-address cards. OK, you get such a card and change your mark's address. It would be good if you had his mail sent to another state. Don't get exotic, though; keep it simple. Use a larger city, like Los Angeles, since this increases the likelihood of further screw-ups as the mark attempts to straighten out the mess when he discovers his mail is no longer arriving. You can double the trouble by changing both home and business addresses. Stop a few moments and think how fouled up your own life would be if your mail was suddenly diverted and possibly lost. It's just a thought. . . .

The Power Cartel

When Metropolitan Edison had to raise money shortly after being embarrassed by its nuclear tinker toy at Three Mile Island in Pennsylvania, the premier psychic semiologist Doctor John McManmon joked that they offered to sell used matches as an alternative power source.

In a far more deadly vein, Eddie Gast doesn't regard the giant utility companies as public services. He sees them as powerful monopolies who buy legislators, judges, and commission officials as human investments toward larger profits for the big stockholders.

"They don't deserve mere dirty tricks," says Gast. "Out-and-out sabotage is all they understand. The ecotage raiders had the answer—cut power lines and blow up towers."

Gast also advocates shooting insulators, trashing vehicles and other power-company equipment, and terrorizing their service workers.

"I also show people how to doctor their home meters to cut way back on the amount of money paid for electricity. Anyone can learn how—a guy even has a book out on it [John Williams, *Stopping Power Meters*, available from Loompanics]. Do unto them before they do unto you, I say."

Asked if this doesn't inconvenience and even hurt

innocent people, Gast says it does, but they must learn who the enemy really is.

Other tricksters are less radical. Osborn Milteer suggests that most of the tricks pulled on the telephone and oil companies will work as well on the power giants.

"Leave the small rural co-ops alone, though," says Milteer.

Surprisingly, Gast agrees, adding, "The rural co-ops are the way things should work. The people really do own them. I want to destroy the mammoth corporations—the monopolies who own nuclear plants and oil companies and act as if they own our government, too."

For example, J. W. Burke, Jr., writes from Virginia to explain the monopoly between the State Corporation Commission and the VEPCO (the Virginia Power Company). He explains that in the middle of May 1979 VEPCO filed for a rate increase of nine million dollars citing financial losses caused by the temporary shutdown of two nuclear units by the federal government. They had already just had a huge increase in March. Without a whimper, the Virginia "regulatory" agency gave in.

According to Burke, that's not the end. Less than a week after getting that nine million, the VEPCO powers came around again asking for an additional nine million.

A mite upset, Burke exploded, "They [VEPCO] don't give a shit about public relations, and they don't need to, because the newspapers here won't even squeak about this. VEPCO also has the State Corporation Commission in their pocket.

"It's worth noting that the SCC has *never* turned down a VEPCO rate-increase request. We have a *lot* of getting even to do here in the Old Dominion."

The power cartel is as vulnerable to the same getting-even tricks as are deserving institutions and persons mentioned in other sections of this book.

Printer

You've noticed that a friendly, trustworthy, and perhaps devious printer has been your staunch associate in so many tricks. A printer can be your best friend, and having access to one or more totally trusted printers is an absolute must for a trickster. There is an old axiom about the printing business that goes, "We don't read the writing; we just set the type." Don't trust it. Instead, trust a friendly printer you know. Often it is easy to find a printer who thinks as you do. If not, your best bet is among large printshops in other cities. Although this is risky, many really don't censor your jobs. But you're better off to cultivate your own good offset printer.

Unless your printer is also a good graphic artist, don't rely on him or her for such services as double printing, counterfeiting official documents, retouching, or sophisticated design work. That work calls for a person who has the specific skills and knowledge to handle it. I might add that those skills are not all that tough to pick up. Speaking from experience, a solid background in advertising and publications work will give you the specific knowledge and skills.

Railroads

If a railroad line has been nasty to you and you want to get back, you are welcome to follow "Bart's" advice. A fan of Edward Abbey, "Bart" offers you the following from his trickster's arsenal. Set the manual brakes on railroad cars; this will cause a great deal of delay in checking and rechecking, which ties up people, time, and money. You can visit the railyard areas on cold, cold nights in winter and pour lots of water on the switch points. This freezes the switches, making them inoperable.

Rats

Here's one where the price just has to be about right. You invest a few dollars in some Norwegian rats—the big, dirty, mean ones. The idea is to get males and females. Put them in some well-screened rabbit hutches. Feed them on garbage and swampweeds. These rodents are cheap to keep, they multiply quickly, and they make people really unhappy. Ask a New Yorker about the Rat Raids of summer 1979! I am sure the imaginations of many readers have already figured out creative things to do with all those rats. Good old Willard, revisited!

Religion

If your mark is a religious sort, you could follow the advice of Lee H. Blakey, who suggests printing up phony letterheads using your mark's name, address, and telephone number under the imprinteur of a group such as Atheists for a Stronger America or Nonbelievers Against God or Gays Against God.

Blakey continues, "You then mail really bitchy letters to local TV stations demanding equal time to make up for 'Sunrise Sermonette.' You also write letters to local newspapers. Sometimes, smaller newspapers don't verify letters that come in on letterheads and are typed well."

From one of my regular religious correspondents, the Reverend Fleisher McGeary, I learned that hooligans have been carrying on near his parish in Packer, Alabama. It seems their trick is to call or visit one of the local whacko religious sects—the goofier and more Holy Roller the better—and ask them to come meditate with "you" and your family. Of course, you give them the name and address of your mark. Another variant is to suggest that the holy folks roll in during the mark's office hours and save the staff. Getting the fix set up here requires a great acting job, lots of sincerely pious rhetoric, and all that glop. But according to McGeary, it works.

If the mark is not well-known in his/her neighborhood, you can call, using the mark's name, and say you would like to come talk with the neighbor about communism, gay rights, gun control, interracial sex relations, or free drugs. The idea here is to be as obnoxious as possible about the issues. Say that your mark represents his/her local church.

If the mark is a Grand Liberal, you can use the same tactic, but turn the topics around—support for the death penalty for most any crime, even tougher antidrug laws, outlawing abortion, and making the ERA illegal.

Restaurants

It used to be annoying when a waitress accidentally stuck her thumb in your soup while serving you lunch. That was before topless waitresses, however.

Suppose you're really fried with a local eatery for charging you for terrible food time after time, and are ready to wash your hands of the whole place. Try silver nitrate instead. If you can introduce a bit of that chemical into the soap dispenser in the restaurant washroom, you will have customers and employees furious with the restaurant. Silver nitrate will leave their hands and faces unwashably stained to an ugly, erratic brown color. It does not come off easily.

Harry Katz, a prominent Pennsylvania socialite, frequents many posh dining establishments in the company of equally ritzy jet setters. He insists that this scam is only a practical joke, which may be correct. However, with a bit of malice aforethought, someone could easily create a nasty version. Harry carries with him a supply of elegantly printed cards. He spots someone he wishes to hassle and bribes a waiter to carry one of the cards over to the mark. The card reads, "The management requests that you and your party leave immediately before we have to call the authorities."

Of course, we don't always have to be so sophisticated. If there are entire groups of people you don't like, you can always eat in restaurants frequented by such people and put salt into the sugar dispensers or unscrew the tops of the salt and pepper shakers, so that the next diner gets a plate full of seasoning. Of course, such stunts are perilously close to April Fool amateurism, but they do have some minor harassment value.

If you had a friend who would take care of the tab, you'd take that friend out to dinner, right? In some swanky and excellent eatery, order your finest repast. Treat yourself to the best. About halfway through the meal, you introduce that friend who's going to take care of your tab. Your friend is a dead cockroach that you brought in with you, carried carefully in your jacket pocket. Place your late friend amid some food on your plate and then turn on your theatrics. Make a noisy fuss and express concern about your health and the restaurant's cleanliness standards, and mutter about your lawyer filing an action. After this, let the management talk you into a free meal or two and some drinks.

This next trick will costs a few bucks, but if you consider it as a perverted investment, the return will be worth many times the outlay. For example, a small display ad could be run in either a campus newspaper or one of the small local newspapers or shoppers. Pick one that isn't too professional, since they are less likely to check the veracity of the ad.

The ad promises some fantastic dinner bargain, such as a steak dinner for two at half price, when the clipped ad is presented between 6 and 7 o'clock that night. Or promise an All You Can Eat Special of roast steamship round of beef for three dollars, with all the trimmings, also with the clipped ad. Use the logo of the restaurant with which you are feuding in the ad. Check their regular ads so your layout looks authentic. Take it in and tell them you're the new assistant who handles advertising. Just don't spend too much time talking or getting remembered. Be prepared to pay cash if necessary.

Between 6 and 7 P.M. your mark will literally have his

restaurant crammed with very hungry and soon-to-be-very-unhappy customers. By 8 P.M. the owner could have a whole lot of ex-customers and an undeserved bad reputation that will be hard to overcome. Or the owner may decide to go along with the "promise," which will cost her/him a lot of bucks. Finally, there will be an unpleasant scene with the newspaper. This scam will also work with local radio stations.

Note, too, that this scam can be turned so that the mark is the newspaper or radio station.

Rubber Stamps

A stock of "official" rubber stamps is an important part of documenting authentication. A good sampling of what you need and what is available may be found in *The New Paper Trip*, a valuable reference book for the dirty trickster. Most office-supply stores and many mail-order outfits sell just about any rubber stamp you need. You will need rubber stamps.

Sleepy Time

If you want your mark to sleep for a bit you should know that the fabled Mickey Finn, knockout drops of grade-B-film fame, is a very real item that you can incorporate into your dirty tricks. The mysterious liquid is simply chloral hydrate. Although it is no longer in general use as a sedative, it is still available. In addition, you can easily find the formula to produce your own version. It's a bitter substance, so mix one gram with several dissolved saccharine tablets before serving. Most experts also suggest that you use the chloral hydrate in connection with booze—a very potent combination.

Another sleepy-time mixture is one capsule of Seconal mixed in with the mark's beer. But as Doctor Christopher Garwood Doyle cautions, use only one capsule and never use this drug with someone who is really loaded or otherwise medically messed up. Seconal is a powerful downer and can be deadly.

Other than that, according to Doyle, you take one capsule of Seconal, the hundred-milligram size, and empty it into a glass of beer. Stir gently and serve to the mark. Sleep will take him away in about fifteen minutes.

Sweet dreams.

Security

Mort Sahl once pointed out that people who were afraid of ideas and thinking would label him an outlaw. Yet Sahl, who has a hell of a lot more understanding and conscience than many people have brains, says he thinks of himself as a moral sheriff. I think we can tie onto that.

Any person concerned with security needs a supply of chains, locks, cables, and glues. Sometimes you need to protect your mark. That might mean chaining his/her car to the bumper of another car at a party, in a parking lot, or on the street. A good padlock completes the picture, and by the time you get some expert there to release things, everyone is unhappy. If your mark is the obvious target, then all the other victims are unhappy with him/her, too.

Locks, chains, and cables are great for closing lanes and driveways, sealing vehicles in or out. They can keep people in offices, homes, apartments, or even buildings. They can fasten objects to other objects. The horizon of your own ideas is not yet even in sight.

Slingshots

Slingshots are useful tools for the dirty trickster. The modern ones are as different from the forked-limb-and-inner-tube variety of your youth as a Daisy BB gun is from a Taser. They aren't even called slingshots any more. The technocrats have renamed them hand catapults. I bet Goliath is turning over in his grave.

Any good sporting-goods store can outfit you with the proper nylon-and-steel Hand Catapult to carry on your missions. If you'd prefer to deal through the mail, write to Wham-O, Box 4, San Gabriel, California 91778. If you want a giant assault model, there's one available, according to Mike Hoy of Loompanics. Mike reports that an outfit known as Information Unlimited, Milford, New Hampshire 03055, sells plans for a "giant slingshot," which is five feet tall and anchored into the ground.

I recall some of the boys in my old neighborhood using an improvised version of the giant slingshot to propel large fruits and vegetables against the home of the neighborhood grouch. They used the fork of a walnut tree and an entire inner tube. A winch drew back the pouch, which could load several cantaloupes, pieces of watermelon, a half dozen tomatoes, or combinations of the above. Effective hits were scored at about 75 yards, as I recall. Perhaps this technique could be put to modern use by means of a mobile weapon.

Stickers

John Hansen of Boulder, Colorado, takes a more passive but no less creative approach in his revenge.

"Vexed by poor service in restaurants, vending machines, and other devices or institutions that take your money and don't deliver the promised services?" Hansen asks. His response is called Creative Revenge.

He has had permastick slogans printed to slap on an offender's premises or equipment. For example, if a vending machine fails to deliver, Hansen slaps it with a sticker reading, THIS MACHINE STEALS MONEY. For restaurants, Hansen has stickers that read, HORRIBLE FOOD, or LOUSY SERVICE. The stickers can be placed on the table or counter, or on the windows and doors of the establishment.

His other stickers include THIS MOVIE RATED BLAH for questionable cinematic efforts, MY TAXES PAID FOR *THIS*? To be placed on examples of government or public foolishness, FILTHY RESTROOMS, for either food-service or gasoline stations, and INEPT NURD for offending civil servants or irritating store clerks.

For the simpleminded who park stupidly in one or more spaces, Hansen tags their vehicles with WAY TO PARK, ACE. He has a bunch of NO MORE JUNK MAIL—RETURN TO SENDER stickers to affix to people's mailboxes. Enraged by the oil companies, John Hansen printed a new sticker for the first time in mid-1979—PRICE GOUGER—which adorns hundreds of service-station gasoline pumps. In many cases, equally irritated station owners are not removing the stickers.

Hansen has a huge variety of stickers, including examples such as RIPOFF; PAID UNDER PROTEST; YES I MIND, DON'T SMOKE; RUDE DRIVER; GAS HOG; and an entire selection of adult stickers that feature hilariously nasty slogans whose R rating places them out of Family Hour. I have used Hansen's stickers, and they are wonderful. For a worthwhile sample kit, send $1 to Consumer Comments, Box 175, Niwot, Colorado 80544.

Supermarkets

Oswald Rankin doesn't like large supermarket chains. He has a favorite game he plays with them, using a least favorite acquaintance as an unwitting accomplice. Ossie explains his game.

"I go the bulletin board of a store out of my neighborhood and remove a policy notice from the bulletin board, since the statement is usually printed on corporate letterhead. At home, I cut off the letterhead and with rubber cement, dummy up a blank piece of paper under it to create a new blank piece of letterhead. I take this to a self-operated coin photocopy machine and get a few good copies that are as clean as the original with no smears or lines showing.

"I call the corporation and learn who a couple of the vice-presidents are by name. Then I type, very carefully and professionally, using a rental electric typewriter at the local library, a very nice letter to several of my least favorite acquaintances. I tell each of them they have won some fabulous prize at their neighborhood store . . . like a small color TV set or two hundred dollars' worth of free groceries, something like that. I tell them they should come in Saturday and claim their prize. I sign the VP's name and mail the bogus letter.

"They show up, and the local store manager is puzzled. He doesn't know what to do. It's Saturday, and he can't call the corporate headquarters. What does he tell the customers? Will they get upset with him? With the store? What do you think happens Monday? And beyond?"

Happy Shopping, Oswald Rankin.

If you're upset by a large corporation that owns a dairy, here's an old trick milk truck drivers used to pull on each other a few years back, before the mammoth agricorporations destroyed competition. The driver for, say, the Udderly Sweet Dairy used a medical syringe to inject a few squirts of lemon concentrate into the milk containers of the Joyful Jugs Dairy. The customer who bought Joyful Jug milk would find the product sour as soon as she/he opened the container and would storm back to the supermarket to sour their corporate milk. It doesn't take too many stormy customers for a supermarket to dump all over a dairy.

Today, of course, medical syringes are only a little bit tougher to obtain, lemon concentrate is easily available, and delivery men don't do this to each other any more because their bosses are all paid by the same international holding corporation. But you aren't and can.

I once interviewed a supermarket manager for an article I wrote on shoplifting. I wanted to find out whether Homer Husband and Harriet Housewife were boosting expensive food as a response to zooming price increases. The very first words out of his mouth were, "Ahhh, we refer to that sort of activity as 'inventory shrinkage' in this business."

Whatever they call it, a lot of people are doing it.

Abbie Hoffman has some interesting ways of stealing from markets that have been targeted for whatever reason:

●   Empty out a pound box of the cheapest margarine you can find and fill it back up with four sticks of the best butter in the store.

●   Sew a drop bag inside your overcoat to receive cuts of meat. Don't be greedy; you don't want to look too bulky.

●   Two or three phonograph records can be placed inside one of those large frozen-pizza boxes.

● Fake an epileptic seizure while your partner, who has already cleaned out the meat counter, flees during the confusion.

● According to Hoffman, stolen food tastes a lot better than store-bought.

Swimming Pools

If your mark has a swimming pool all sorts of additives and accessories are available for your incursion into a targeted recreation area. Dyes are a good choice, and there are many chemicals available to do the job. Placing colored dye in the water could create quite an expensive maintenance problem. Heavy doses of salt will create difficulty for your mark, as will fertilizer and the bacteria-inducing chemicals sold for septic systems.

Another swimming-pool additive you could consider is an extract of toxicodendrol, which is the nonvolatile oil found in the poison-ivy plant so memorable to legions of its fans from experiences in camping, fishing, picnicking, loving, or whatever. If you've had a brush with poison ivy, you can easily imagine what the concentrated extract could do if introduced into the mark's swimming pool.

It's not very creative, but you could put dead animals in his/her pool. That's why you should always keep several large trash or lawn plastic bags in your car—you never know when you're going to happen upon an especially disgusting piece of roadkill. Generally, for swimming pools, the larger the dead animal you can manage to get into the mark's pool the better. Call the zoo; maybe they'll give you their next dead elephant. Use a fictitious name and have the animal sent to a safe mail drop!

Some of my acquaintances belong to esoteric military units like Special Forces, SEALS, Blue Light, etc. One of them recently told me about a non-issue application of the orange dye marker solution that is normally issued for air-sea rescue work.

My friend recalled, "It happened down South, when we were refused membership in a community swimming pool because (1) we were military types and (2) two of our five were black dudes. Since these civilian bozos were so color conscious, we decided to give the locals some sensitivity training.

"A friend in Supply got us some orange dye marker, and a week or so later we pulled a late-night recon mission into enemy territory. We loaded up their lily-white pool with orange dye. Man, does that stuff work—even better than we thought! It messed up the filters and pumps something fierce, and it coated the bottom and sides of the pool this vivid orange. Oh yeah, the whole pool full of water was ruined too.

"This made local TV coverage, and were the city fathers pissed off! They figured it was us military types, but nobody had any courtroom proof. The local hoods were afraid to mess with us physically, so the whole thing was a draw. It cost them a few thousand bucks to get the pool running again. By then, we'd discovered we could enjoy the base pool anyway. That was our contribution to making some bigots a bit less discriminatory."

Teachers

Early one morning before their teacher got to the classroom, some students painted a large black/brown spot on the ceiling. With some deft art touches, it looked as if a huge hole had suddenly broken through. They piled broken plaster, ceiling wire, and hunks of lath on the floor beneath the hole.

The teacher was a priss, and when he came in and saw the mess he pranced out to inform the principal. Quickly, the perpetrators cleaned the water paint off the ceiling and swept up the floor. They disposed of the residue and trash on the roof outside the room.

When the principal and the teacher returned, the students acted innocently concerned about the teacher's sanity. The principal asked the teacher to please stop in and see him at the first available moment. As he left, the principal stared at the teacher for a long, long time.

If you don't like a teacher, here's the ticket, according to that veteran student of human affairs Doug Dedge. You have to get your mark to a library where they use an electronic sensor to catch people taking books out of the place without proper checkout. Locate your mark. Then go to the periodicals section and page through magazines until you locate and remove several of the metallic sensor strips.

Carefully plant these on your mark or on his/her own

books, briefcase, overcoat, or whatever. The idea is to get multiple plantings. Perhaps a diversion could be created to allow you the few seconds needed to plant the sensors. Stick around and enjoy the fun when the mark tries to go out the door.

Your planted sensors will set off the bell. This will cause extreme shock, upset, indignation, and confusion. With luck, only one sensor will be found at first, and the mark will try to leave again. Round two is also yours.

Because teachers deal with children, they are especially susceptible to child-molesting charges, deserved or not. Claude Pendejo's son was accused by his teacher of cheating on a test and given an F. The boy, who was quite innocent, literally cried his innocence. No one believed him but his parents. The teacher was especially insolent about the entire matter, refusing to even talk with the parents. The teachers' union backed their errant member, and that caused the principal to shy away from the case.

Claude Pendejo decided that because this teacher had messed up his son, it was only fitting for the man to become a molester of a different sort.

After giving the teacher a couple of months to forget the incident, Pendejo acted. One morning, each home in the neighborhood around this school was posted with a brief letter, run off on a cheap mimeo machine. The letter stated that the teacher in question had molested the little child of the letter's grieving writer—a scared mother—and only now did this parent have the courage to come forth. The "writer" of the letter said that the teacher had sexually abused her son on four occasions, and finally the pain and shame had made him come to his parents for salvation. The "humble mother" said the police would do nothing, so she, as a frightened mother, was appealing directly to other concerned parents for their help in ridding their neighborhood school of this horrible beast.

Within three days, the man was blamed (wrongly) for an actual molesting incident totally unrelated to the scam. Two other kids came forward and "confessed" he had made sexual advances to them (he had not). The man was waylaid by two fathers and pushed around, his car was trashed, and the neighborhood cop told him he would have his eye on the man. The teacher's wife was a suspicious sort anyway, and this whole thing just fed their marital fires. Finally, his supervisor told the man he was too much of a problem and he ought to consider either moving away or going into a new line of work. This happened after the local paper ran a "guilty or no" story on the whole matter. Since there was no actual proof, the paper was somewhat sympathetic to the mark. Eventually, the whole matter burned down to a few embers of suspicion that would never die out.

Telephones

Until I considered some of my acquaintances as potential marks, I could not believe that this scam was serious, especially since the wonderful humorist H. Allen Smith suggested it. You call your mark, identify yourself as being from the telephone company's service division, and say something like this:

"We're calling to warn you that we're going to be blowing out the telephone lines this afternoon. We advise you to cover your telephone with a plastic bag, and under no circumstances should you use it between the hours of 1 and 4 P.M. If the instrument is not covered you run the risk of having the receiver damaged and of having grease and soot from the lines blown into your home should the receiver be lifted from the phone during this line-cleaning operation. Thank you, blah, blah, blah. . . ."

Smith swore he had personal knowledge that this bit works. That's good enough for me. Have a blowing good time cleaning out someone's telephone line.

This next stunt works best early in the morning, late in the day, or always with some people. Pick out that special jerk and call him/her on the telephone. Here's how to run the conversation.

YOU: Hello, who is this please?

MR. ELDER: This is Mr. Elder.

YOU: Oh, I'm sorry—he's not here right now.

MR. ELDER: What? Who's not there?

YOU: Mr. Elder is not here.

MR. ELDER: Wait a minute, *I'm* Mr. Elder. *You* called—

YOU [*interrupting Mr. Elder*]: I'm sorry, sir—Mr. Elder just [stepped out, is in a meeting, isn't at his desk, etc.] right now. May I have him call you back?

MR. ELDER: You fool, *I* am Mr. Elder. I didn't call him; I *am* him. You made this call. *You* called *me. I'm* Mr. Elder!

YOU: Will you please calm down, sir, and let me have your name and number. I'll have Mr. Elder call you just as soon as he gets back. Actually, he really went across the street to get [a drink, shot up with dope, laid]. We're having some really terrible problems with him.

By now the line will have gone dead. If Mr. Elder doesn't hang up, you should, after the usually cheery and phony "Have a nice day, now." You have gone a long way toward ruining Mr. Elder's day.

Starting at about 2:30 A.M., call the mark's home. When he/she answers, ask for someone, anyone . . . let's say you ask for Dave Rottedgel.

"Dave who?" says the sleepy voice.

"Dave Rottedgel. Is he there?"

The mark growls, "No, you have a wrong number."

About fifteen minutes later, using a different voice or having an associate call, do it again. And again. And again. Always ask for the same person—in this case, Dave Rottedgel. When the caller(s) feel the mark is starting to get really hot and has probably had his or her sleep ruined for that night, it is time for the final call.

"Hello, [use mark's first name]?"

Wearily and probably snappishly, the mark will answer, "Yes, it is."

"Hey, this is Dave Rottedgel. Any calls for me?"

The way to handle wrong numbers in a nasty way is to wait for a few moments of silent effect to build up just after you answer the phone, then laugh as hollowly and mockingly as you can right into the mouthpiece. Never utter a word. Just give 'em that horrible, hollow laugh and hang up. Don't answer the phone if it rings again shortly.

Before taking the vows, Sister Laverne Finneri, of Our Mother of Perpetual Flatulence, used to be a telephone trickster. Her best fun came in calling about two hundred people and hoping that in at least fifty cases, the asked-for party was not home but a message could be taken.

"Thank you, would you please have [name of party to get message] call [name of mark] back any time after midnight tonight. Yes, it is very, *very* important or I wouldn't ask you to have him/her call so late."

Laverne reports that it worked. "I used to check it out by calling the mark's number around 1:30 A.M. Sometimes the line was busy, and sometimes the mark answered and would be almost hysterical."

Professor Joe Berg is an engineer at Wolffie's, Inc., and is also a telephone funster. Here is one of the good professor's ideas.

"Unscrew the mouthpiece on your mark's telephone. Note the metallic contact on the bottom of that loose cylinder with the holes in the top. Spray that contact area with clear paint or coat it with clear nail polish. The idea is to disrupt the electrical contact, which will disable the telephone. It's a very puzzling business to the mark and will cause the repair person some trouble, too."

Theft

Theft and other bits of guerrilla warfare by employees against a despised corporation have long, deep roots. Greedy, embittered, politically alienated, or just plain loose-fingered employees took home an unauthorized twelve billion dollars in 1979. This bit of larceny is so easy and requires so little thought that most experts regard it as little more than another expense of doing business.

"We figure the cost of a certain percentage of employee theft right in with our other costs like rent, advertising, overhead, salaries," says business economist Ivo Neglagenti. "Most companies add this cost right into the amounts they charge the public for goods and services."

Does that mean if you steal from your employer you are simply stealing from yourself? One anti-corporate guerrilla has a ready response: "Simply steal more than your share of the cost. Like the old bromide goes, never steal anything small, and if you do, do it often."

Abbie Hoffman gives you the operational details in his classic *Steal This Book*. Good luck finding it, though. It is apparently "out of theft," and no publisher wishes to reprint it. Try used-book shops. It's an instructive book.

If you're interested in petty larceny, Loran Eugene Braden suggests you experiment with various sizes of brass washers in coin-operated vending machines. If you don't like a particular newspaper, he suggests you use number-fourteen washers in their vending machines, remove all the newspapers, take them into bars and other places, and sell them yourself.

Braden adds. "Hey, even if the washers don't operate the machine there's always the hope they will jam the coin slots. So you don't really lose in any case."

Obviously, some of the radical advocates of rights for ordinary citizens are both preaching and practicing theft as a form of fighting back. I was brought up to believe that stealing is not nice. On the other hand, maybe some of these antiestablishment tactics aren't really stealing. I leave the decision to you.

Most modern philosophers recognize a major difference between theft for fun, for survival, for a career, and for protest purposes. As the premier corrections officer Wallace R. Croup points out, "A common thief will steal from anyone, whereas a protestor will steal only from his institutional enemy—a corporation, utility, or some other establishment target."

Even so, maybe you still have a moral block about theft. If so, think how thin the dividing line is between business as usual and stealing. Some of the Detroit auto companies know that their products are dangerous death traps; yet they sell them anyway. You pay nine dollars for a tiny container of a prescription drug. Do you really believe that the compound costs that much? Talk to a salesperson for a large drug company if you doubt me. I wish you could see the breakdown of costs in producing laundry detergent. I worked in advertising. I saw those figures, and know how many dollars you have to pay for how few cents' worth of materials and labor.

There is a *very* thin line between business and theft.

Toilets

If you enjoy playing in the potty without blowing one up, consider this trick. Saturate a large dry sponge with a thick starch solution. Squeeze it tightly into a ball and tie it down as tightly as possible with tough string. Allow the whole thing to dry thoroughly. Then remove the string, and the sponge will stay in its compressed state. Pop it, or as many as you've made, into targeted toilets, flush the sponge down, and walk away from the fun.

It may take a while for the sponge to become wet enough to expand solidly. Have patience—it will do so soon. For your purposes, you probably hope it is farther down the drainage system than is convenient for a repairperson to get to easily. Holy backup!

If you have some of that poison-ivy extract left over from the section on swimming pools, heed Ed Hoover's story. As a kid, Ed obtained some extract of toxicodendrol (poison ivy) and applied it liberally to the toilet paper in the counselors' outhouse at his summer camp. He said he later did the same thing to the officers' latrine while serving Uncle Sam. Maybe Ed just has this problem with authority figures. Even so, that's a lot more comfortable than the problems his authority figures got wiped out with.

Mower McMurphy sticks closely to commodes. Like the sticker man from Boulder, McMurphy has a very sharp, nasty mind and uses creative revenge. One of his classics is to have official-looking warnings printed on permastick stock. When, for some reason, he gets irritated at someone or something in a bar, office building, school, or utility, he will post each restroom stall in the area.

Each sticker bears an official-looking seal and signature around the message, which reads: DANGER: THIS RESTROOM OFF-LIMITS DUE TO INFECTIOUS VENEREAL DISEASE. STAY OUT FOR YOUR OWN HEALTH PROTECTION.

In another campaign, McMurphy printed up graffiti-style stickers, which he posted over toilet-paper dispensers in the bathrooms of least-favorite marks. The stickers read: WARNING: THIS TOILET PAPER HAS BEEN INFECTED WITH A HIGHLY CONTAGIOUS NEW STRAIN OF ASIAN GONORRHEA. Uh-huh—I know what you're thinking. But, would you really take the chance anyway?

Now, if you wish to be discriminatory, this next trick works best in a bathroom frequented by women. According to nationally known sexist Butch Bryant, it is also an old trick—cheap bathroom humor, Butch calls it. A gay sort, though, Butch will always settle for a laugh. Butch once said, "A cheap thrill is better than no thrill."

Lift the seat of the commode, then stretch and place Saran Wrap very tightly across the top of the bowl so no creases show. Then lower the seat gently. The trap is set.

Ideally, the mark will come dashing in, sit, and let loose. Your humorous imagination can finish the rest of this trick, when the trap is sprung, so to speak. Butch Bryant says this works best in barroom johns. Anything you say, Butch.

La Turista

If your mark is traveling into Mexico or some South or Central American country, or even into Canada, you could consider doing your duty as an honorable citizen and reporting your suspicions to the authorities of that country that he/she is a drug dealer. It might help to sneak some drugs into the mark's car, luggage, or clothing prior to his or her hitting a border point. If you are kindhearted you will have the discovery made on the U.S. side of the border. If not? Hey, this is only a book. It's his/her life.

VIP

We've all tried to get that always unavailable very Important Person Who Can Solve Our Problem on the telephone. But that Important Person always is tied up, is in a meeting, or just stepped out of the office. So after you waste your time calling him or her in vain a few times, do it yet one more time.

This time come armed with the name of the chief executive officer of the company. Get that from the main switchboard operator. When the unavailable Very Important Person's flunky starts to give you the runaround again, sternly tell the flunky something like this:

"I didn't want to bring [use full name of chief executive] into this little matter. I thought your [use name of very important person here] could handle this him/herself. I guess not. Well, I'm calling [first name of chief executive] for a luncheon soon, and I can just ask him/her about this matter then."

No person wants the superior, especially the chief executive, to think that he/she is incapable of handling routine matters. Beyond that, the fact that you have namedropped adds a dimension few bureaucratic managers care to call as a bluff. It's easier and cheaper to finally talk to you—and satisfy you.

Water Wells

People who live outside the lines of municipal services provide their own utilities, one of which is a water well. Normally, these wells are topped by a simple metal cap held in place by several set screws. It takes only a few minutes to loosen the screws, remove the cap, and dump a load of modest-sized roadkill, such as squirrels, small rabbits, rats, birds, etc., down the well casing. Replace the cap and tighten the screws, and the mark will be none the wiser. For a while.

Water wells are usually purified once a year by adding a gallon of a chlorine bleach, such as Clorox, to the well. This process also oxidizes the iron in the water, turning the liquid a dirty, rusty color. The water now stinks and tastes awful. To demolish the quality of your mark's water supply for at least a week, dump about ten to fifteen gallons of bleach down the well.

Barfo Renchquist got his nickname as you might imagine. His favorite water-well trick is to eat all sorts of multi-colored greasy junk food, like pizza. He drinks a lot of beer, too. Primed and loaded, he is driven to the mark's water well. The well cap is removed, and Barfo positions himself over the well casing and pulls his trigger by sticking his finger down his throat. Barfo does his thing— all of it down the well. The well cap is replaced.

"It works best when they don't have too fine a filter on their pump and some of the small pieces of puke come out the house taps. A lot of the color, smell, and taste almost always comes through. It's a very demoralizing stunt," Barfo reports.

Wills

If you have a least-favorite friend, relative, or other family member you want to shame in front of the others, write him/her into your last will and testament. Simply instruct your attorney to include a codicil to the effect that "I bequeath all my yachts, silver plate, gold bullion and coins, foreign holdings, carriages, and aircraft to [name of mark]." Obviously, you had best not have any of those items, or you suddenly *become* the mark. This stunt is a blow from the grave. Maybe you won't know how it works. Maybe, though, you will. Is there revenge after death?

Bibliography

Abbey, Edward. *The Monkey Wrench Gang*. Philadelphia: Lippincott, 1975.

Alexander, Alfred. *Stealing*. New York: Cornerstone, 1966.

Army, Department of. *Booby Traps* (FMS-31). Washington: HQ, U.S. Army, 1965.

————. *Unconventional Warfare Devices and Techniques* (TM 31-200-1). Boulder: Paladin, 1970 (reprint).

Bern, Major H. von Dach. *Total Resistance.* Boulder: Paladin, 1965.

Berne, Eric. *Games People Play*. New York: Grove, 1964.

Blackstock, Norman. *COINTELPRO*. New York: Vintage, 1975

Charell, Ralph. *How I turn Ordinary Complaints into Thousands of Dollars*. New York: Stein and Day, 1973.

————. *How to Get the Upper Hand*. New York: Stein and Day, 1978.

Confidential Publications. *A Remail Service* (available from Loompanics).

Felknor, Bruce. *Dirty Politics*. New York: Norton, 1966.

French, Scott. *The Big Brother Game*. Secaucus, N.J.: Lyle Stuart, 1975.

Guevara, Che. *Guerrilla Warfare*. New York: Vintage, 1961.

Hapgood, David. *The Screwing of the Average Man*. New York: Doubleday, 1974.

————. *The Average Man Fights Back*. Doubleday, 1977.

Herzog, Arthur. *The B.S. Factor: Theory and Technique of Faking It in America*. Baltimore: Penguin, 1970.

Hoffman, Abbie. *Revolution for the Hell of It*. New York: Penguin, 1970.

————. *Steal This Book*. New York: Pirate Editions, 1971.

Hoy, Michael. *Loompanics Unlimited*. Loompanics Unlimited, Box 264, Mason, Michigan 48854. This is the best catalog of its kind in the world. A dirty trickster cannot be without this valuable reference tool.

Hyde, H. Montgomery. *Room 3603*. New York: Farrar, Straus, 1962.

Levy, Bert. *Guerrilla Warfare*. Boulder: Paladin, 1964.

Lukas, J. Anthony. *Nightmare*. New York: Viking, 1976.

Matthews, Douglas. *Yes, You Can Sue the Bastards*. New York: Dell, 1975.

Nichols, John. *The Milagro Beanfield War*. New York: Ballantine, 1976.

Office of Strategic Services. *OSS Sabotage and Demolitions Manual*. Boulder: Paladin, 1974 (reprint).

Patterson, William. *Detective, Private Investigating Manual*. Boulder: Paladin, 1979.

Powell, William. *The Anarchist Cookbook*. Secaucus, N.J.: Lyle Stuart, 1971.

Reid, Barry. *The New Paper Trip*. Fountain Valley, California: Eden, 1979.

Rosner, Joseph. *The Hater's Handbook*. New York: Delacorte, 1965

Rubin, Jerry. *Do It*. New York: Simon & Schuster, 1970.

Sahl, Mort. *Heartland*. New York: Harcourt, 1976.

Santoro, Victor *Techniques of Harassment,* volume 1 and volume 2. Cornville, Arizona: Desert, 1979.

Saxon, Kurt. *The Poor Man's James Bond*. Eureka, California: Atlan Formularies, 1972.

Smith, H. Allen. *The Compleat Practical Joker*. New York: Doubleday, 1953.

Stevenson, William. *A Man Called Intrepid*. New York: Harcourt, 1976.

Striker, John, and Shapiro, Andrew. *Superthreats*. New York: Rawson, 1977.

Tinker, Scot. *The Con Series* (available from Loompanics).

Townsend, Robert. *Up the Organization*. New York: Crest, 1970.

Wasserman, Harvey. *Energy War: Reports from the Front*. Westport, Connecticut: Lawrence Hill, 1979.